MISTER FRANCHISE

MISTER FRANCHISE

David B. Slater

Mister Franchise
Copyright © 2014 David B. Slater

All rights reserved. No part of this book may be reproduced (except for inclusion in reviews), disseminated or utilized in any form or by any means, electronic or mechanical, including photocopying, recording, or in any information storage and retrieval system, or the Internet/World Wide Web without written permission from the author or publisher.

For more information e-mail the author: dslater6@verizon.net

Printed in the United States of America

Mister Franchise
David B. Slater

1. Title   2. Author   3. Business

Library of Congress Control Number: 2013920860

ISBN 13: 978-0-615-91899-0

*This book is dedicated to my wife, Barbara, and our five sons.
Without them there would be no Mister Franchise.*

Table of Contents

Foreword ix

Introduction
Becoming Mister Franchise: Stumbling into a Lifelong Passion and Career xiii

Franchising Fundamentals 1

The History of Franchising 19

A Potpourri 37

Finding a Franchise That Fits Like a Glove 53

Show Me the Money 69

Creating a Business Plan 81

Running a Franchise 105

Growing as a Franchisee 131

Conclusion 147

Foreword
by Jonathan S. Slater

While I'm not a religious person, I have generally regarded the Ten Commandments as a good thing, especially those parts about murder, theft, adultery, and coveting thy neighbor's wife. However, I haven't really focused on the fifth commandment: "honor thy father and mother." Perhaps that's because my parents have made it so easy for us. As the oldest of five sons, I know it's been easy for me, and I know each of my brothers feels the same way. Our parents are amazing people and have set wonderful examples. We've been very fortunate.

But this book isn't about parenting (maybe that will be the sequel). It's about my father as a businessman, and it's about franchising, a subject in which he is a preeminent expert. As the oldest child, I've have had the unique privilege of spending a lot of time in business with my father , starting in high school, when I would accompany him often to meetings and even on trips. The subject didn't matter; I was there at his side, and we'd discuss those meetings extensively both before and after. It was the best apprenticeship I could imagine.

During the summer of my junior year at Stanford, I worked for my father in franchise sales at ABC Mobile Brake in Los Angeles, a wholesale brake-repair franchise that then had about three hundred units operating nationally. During that time I got to sell my first franchise on my own. I remember flying out to Minneapolis, staying at the Pfister Hotel, and pitching prospects from the room on the advantages of owning an ABC Mobile Brake franchise. It was a heady experience at such a young age, and I was thrilled to be able to make my father proud.

Also in college I spent a lot of time exploring potential acquisition opportunities with my father, at one point focusing on cookie-store franchises. (Coincidentally Mrs. Fields' first store was in downtown Palo Alto, and we all got an early firsthand look at how good a good cookie store could be.) Ultimately my father set his sights on a 250-unit chain called The American Cookie Company. After negotiating the potential purchase for approximately $15 million, we flew to Chicago to meet with Jay Pritzker, the wealthy conglomerateer of Hyatt Hotel fame (among lots of other businesses). I knew Mr. Pritzker, who once had tried to buy Mister Donut, had great respect for my father's business skills and judgment.

The meeting was organized on an impromptu basis and occurred while Mr. Pritzker got a haircut in the barbershop at the Standard Club in Chicago. It's almost comical to imagine: Mr. Pritzker in one chair, my father in another, and I in the third. At the end of the meeting/haircut, Mr. Pritzker stood up and gave my father the green light, although my father ultimately turned down the deal—it seemed the cookies just weren't good enough, and the company had grown too quickly with too many bad stores. I think this decision to reject the acquisition enhanced Mr. Pritzker's admiration for my father; fifteen years later we approached him to reacquire Mister Donut from International Multifoods, and he gave us a blank check. Unfortunately we ultimately lost a bidding war with Allied Domecq, which owned Dunkin' Donuts and had a big advantage because of their ability to eliminate virtually all of Mister Donut's corporate overhead.

At twenty-three I left a high-powered job on Wall Street in aerospace finance to join my father in the management of Omnidentix, the first large-scale chain of franchised group dental offices. Omnidentix was visionary, as the success of large dental chains like Aspen Dental attest to today; unfortunately it was about fifteen years before its time. Back then the federal government and about fifteen states had entered the franchise regulation business, requiring the preparation and submission of extensive franchise disclosure documents. Naturally my father, as a lawyer and the first chairman of the Legal Committee of the International Franchise Association, of which he was also a cofounder, was ahead of the game on this front: he wrote all our franchise agreements and many of our initial state registration applications.

Ultimately he passed this knowledge on to me. I wrote and updated many others and actually became somewhat of a franchising expert in my own right. We sold upward of thirty-five dental franchises in about ten states from the Northeast to Florida to Illinois. While the company was prospering on many fronts, dental recruiting was a bit of an obstacle given the stigma then associated with working for group practices. Of course this is no longer the case, which shows what a difference the right timing makes. Omnidentix was ultimately victimized by corporate politics as the CEO of our financing source changed, and the new guy opted to pull the plug on our growth capital, causing the company to be sold to a competitor. While that CEO subsequently apologized for this ill-informed decision (I'm not sure he ever really knew much about the company), it's scary how reckless people can be with other people's money. But that's probably fodder for another book.

Anyway, what training I had. The opportunities and responsibility afforded me by growing up alongside and working for my father were amazing. These experiences explain why I was so well prepared for the case-study program at Harvard Business School—because I had lived so many cases firsthand, dealing with all facets of business from marketing to sales to finance to operations to human resources. I'll always treasure the opportunities we had to work together and lament the fact that those opportunities didn't last longer.

My father served as the inspiration for two of the businesses I started after business school and my subsequent successful career in M&A on Wall Street. He was there at the inception of SmarTel, a phone-card business I started and then built and sold for $10 million the mid- to late 1990s. My father scouted out the initial opportunity and was invaluable as a mentor and chairman of our board of directors. Similarly he provided the idea behind AmeriCounsel.com, an Internet legal services portal I also started and built. This was yet another idea before its time, as the success of Legal Zoom now demonstrates approximately ten years later.

Common among all my father's undertakings was the vision to identify unmet opportunities, the ability to galvanize resources to create something from nothing, and the leadership to direct others through unchartered waters.

We all have a lot to learn from David Slater, Mister Franchise. Thank you, Dad.

Introduction

Becoming Mister Franchise: Stumbling into a Lifelong Passion and Career

Do you dream of walking away from your current job to finally become your own boss? If you have a burning passion to own your own business but would like to reduce the risks and liabilities of starting one by yourself then owning a franchise is for you. If you have some capital and credit, this book will show you how; it is based on over fifty years of my own personal franchising experiences since the birth of the franchising industry.

I graduated from law school in 1959, was on Law Review, and passed the Massachusetts Bar before serving in the army as a lieutenant then working as a defense attorney and later a prosecutor. What mother wouldn't have been proud?

So you can imagine how upset she was (she had been the valedictorian of her large high school class) when I returned to my native Boston the next year and, instead of practicing law, began franchising from the first three original Mister Donut shops. I had to explain to my mother over and over again that I was not going into the donut business just to run these shops but rather was putting other people into their own donut business under a Mister Donut franchise. I enthusiastically invested all my energy and passion into this new form of business expansion that had very little precedent: franchising.

It was difficult to explain to Mom since even McDonald's and KFC were still brand-new ideas, blazing an unprecedented path as they quickly grew. We were pioneers of this new frontier, and everything we did was best defined as management by accident. I thought I could offset a lot of the disadvantages of my young age with a law degree and the knowledge of contracts, real estate, financing, and other necessary and beneficial legal background for this new business-growth system. Although competition quickly grew fierce, it was a new concept, not really yet an industry, and there were not yet experienced executives.

I thought that my chance of success was fairly good, and I was reasonably confident. I had a great education and won my cases in the military, including one I was assigned to at the adjoining air force base for a front-page news bribery defense. And I realized that if franchising didn't work out as well as I hoped, I could easily switch to practicing law and even utilize the new knowledge I would have gained.

I had countless unique and amazing experiences, flying by the seat of my pants in the franchising world, learning through trial and error. From the infant days of franchising and Mister Donut, we built a superior management team and grew the chain into a coast-to-coast presence throughout the United States, Canada, and internationally, with some two to three hundred stores.

We had a strategic plan to open fifty to one hundred new stores annually. Expanding to the same size as Dunkin' Donuts, we sold the company to International Multifoods in 1970, when the company grew to approximately fifteen hundred stores. When Mister Donut was sold to Allied Domeque (NYSE), which also owned Dunkin' Donuts, they merged the two companies into a chain of over four thousand stores. Around one thousand Dunkin' Donuts stores today began as Mister Donut franchises. About five hundred others were closed by Dunkin' because they were too close to one of their existing stores or were located in too small a town. Dunkin' Donuts has now set their sights on growing to fifteen thousand shops.

However, things have changed. In the past, a shop with donut sales under 60 percent of revenue was usually unsuccessful. Today, 20 percent of revenue in donuts and bakery products is good. The product mix offered has moved significantly to soups and sandwiches to augment donut and other bakery-product sales such as muffins, bagels, and croissants.

Donuts and these bakery products are now made in a commissary, mostly by machines and not hand cut, and are then distributed to small outlets (without kitchens), gas stations, 7-Elevens, and the like. If sales in these outlets are not profitable, the units are easily moved with little loss.

Then, as a result, with the advent of commissary production utilizing donut-making machines, coupled with their transport to each shop as needed and finished off there as needed (for example, filled or sugar coated), bakers are no longer required in each and every shop. They were and are always hard to hire (their heaviest workload being the large production of donuts in the middle of the night to meet the early morning demand). Since they are harder to find, this was a great concept from the beginning. Today's commissary production technique makes it more profitable and quickly expandable.

Coffee is still a huge factor, and if it could be made to taste better, it certainly would be—but it can't. Believe me—we've experimented in many ways. It is so important that Mister Donut advertised the "World's Best Coffee."

Almost from the start, I realized how lucky I was to have chosen the franchising route. My friends did not have the good fortune to connect with something so immediately explosive as franchising, though they have succeeded in their own chosen fields.

Moving on after Mister Donut, I continued to create new franchises, such as Sizzleboard Restaurants, ABC Mobile Brake Systems, ABC Mobile Muffler, Omnidentix Dental Centers, Smart Talk Promotional Telephone Cards and Americouncil Legal Systems, Franchise Programming and Consulting, and Franchise Executive Recruitment. We also became a franchisee of Yves Saint Laurent's Rive Gauche line, opening their high-end boutiques in Boston; Short Hills, New Jersey; and Dallas.

In addition, for more than thirty years, I operated over fifty group homes for developmentally disabled adults. During its thirty-plus years of operation, the company never earned a positive cash flow, losing in excess of $1.5 million in capital. However, from the start, the intention was to "give back" using the company's chain-store expertise to develop a then-new (as far as anyone could determine) small group home system, contributing to the closing down of the existing huge institutional system—an idea then-governor of Massachusetts Francis Sergeant requested of me.

Fortunately, our franchise consulting business made large financial contributions to the company. We were fortunate to have many clients, the largest among them being Armor and Co., the meat packers. Even before Mutual Enterprises was created, I had been a consultant to WR Grace for a highly successful French acquisition they were considering, which I recommended they make at a special Grace Board of Directors meeting called to consider that acquisition. Grace made many millions on the deal as it later resold their interest. The project featured the development of Howard Johnson-like restaurants and motels, straddling superhighways that were then just being constructed throughout France, similar to those being built in the United States of America.

Our most fun creation, perhaps, was STEAK OUT, one of three franchise concepts we developed for Armor and Co., from the inception of the idea to its graphics, design, operating manuals, and even sample legal documents. It featured a fast-food restaurant for prime locations, walk in or drive in, featuring several types of inexpensive steak sandwiches with numerous add ons, sauces, condiments, and of course potatoes, drinks, and desserts. The motif was cops and robbers, including even the rest rooms. It was concluded that the corniness would be more than offset by all the fun features. Unfortunately, before we could open the first one, Armor was acquired, and the whole project dropped with the others. We were too busy at Mister Donut to do it ourselves.

Finally, as a consolation prize, much of my consulting effort for WR Grace required my presence in Paris. As a result, my wife and I celebrated our tenth anniversary with a two-week stay at one of the world's best hotels in Paris, as guests of WR Grace.

We also owned the nationally franchised car-rental service Airways Rent a Car, the nation's fourth-largest car-rental operation. Later, when we sold it to a cooperative of the existing franchise owners, they were thereafter essentially paying franchise fees to themselves. This business featured several thousand cars, primarily in airports. When we sold it, each dealer had ownership in the co-op, determined by its size. It was the perfect customer since the dealers built their agencies and were part of the ultimate buyers of the chain. In between, they were essentially paying their fees to themselves, making the collection of franchise fees easier. It was also very interesting dealing with the car manufacturers, and they also offered free loaner cars for the management, swapped monthly for new cars. We could have any car we desired, even a Mercedes.

These experiences led to my becoming a founder and initial director of the International Franchise Association and chairman of their legal committee, as well as the founder and chairman of The Boston College Center for Franchise Distribution and its annual Own Your Own Business show.

The deeper I got into writing this book and reminiscing about those good old days, the more I felt like jumping back into the business of franchising and starting up something special again. But hard work, long hours, and what I always referred to as "stick-to-it-iveness" are the keys to success in this form of enterprise. At my age, I decided that perhaps the best thing for me to do is to stay in consulting and not-for-profit efforts, passing along my passion, advice, and enthusiasm in this book, explaining the ins and outs and ups and downs of purchasing a franchise and making it successful, as well as franchising your own business.

So don't procrastinate. Dive right in and investigate franchising and perhaps get in the game. You may never get this chance again, so live your dreams. Invest in *yourself*.

1

Franchising Fundamentals

You're going to have to work somewhere doing something, so consider that one of the most rewarding and enjoyable ways to spend your working life is by being your own boss. Why not own and operate your own business, make your own decisions, and experience the pride of earning a profit for all of your risk and effort? You have the opportunity to build up equity in the business you develop and own, no matter how modest, and someday you can likely sell and maybe even retire on the proceeds from the sale.

Of course you also have the risk of loss, creating anxiety, but you can always go back to working for someone else in the worst-case scenario.

The primary issue, of course, is making a profit and having enough cash flow to pay yourself a decent salary. You will have to put in many hours and much effort, but eventually you will—hopefully—earn a higher profit, one that may even allow you to hire a manager to do much of the work for you.

The key is creating a successful enterprise, and my experience has proven to me that unless you have some special talent, experience, and knowledge, a franchise is a terrific guide. It's not a guarantee, but at a modest price it is a proven opportunity to a profitable business.

Purchasing a franchise is among the best ways to start such a business, offering minimal, more controlled risk than a normal, untried startup. For all practical purposes, you are on your own but not really by yourself. There is an expert franchisor to help guide you down the previously traveled road to success. Yes, it is for a fee, but it is worth paying for the support, knowledge, and experience he or she has already gained. You'll likely spend more (or similar) funds than the franchise fee and the ongoing royalty on the research you would need to do on your own and would probably make countless costly mistakes in the process of learning without the advice you'll get along the way when in operation.

Most of the disadvantages of starting your own business from scratch or operating alone are minimized, but the cost is usually reasonable considering the risk reduction and transfer of knowhow. The franchisors have been there and repeated the process again and again. They have proven time after time that the system they created, improved, adapted, and promoted does in fact work and create profits if executed properly. Indeed, the better it is operated, invariably the better the results.

If you have a similar amount of experience and knowledge, you could well be better off on your own and save the fees, but odds are you do not. For example, if you were a chef at a successful restaurant for an adequate amount of time to gain the necessary knowhow to open and operate your own vision for your eatery, you would not need a franchisor's help. Indeed, most franchisors view experienced franchisees as a negative toward success because they have found that the franchisees that think that their own ways of doing things, gained from their personal experience, are the best or right ways often doesn't follow the system's rules and are usually not good operators. The franchisor's way is proven again and again to be the best. A franchisee's desire to do it his or her own way usually isn't the way the franchisor would want it done and is typically not the best action for that operation.

But those with limited or no experience are significantly better off to follow a franchise model rather than invent a new mold. Work, effort, and attention may be the most important ingredients for success in business, but there are so many avenues and ways to fail that every crutch available is helpful insurance of not just survival but a positive result.

For the average individual, buying a franchise is clearly the best route you can take. It distributes the burdens of overall operations, along with the financial results and rewards proportionately. There is nothing like coupling your work with an investment of your own money to create motivation for success. With this financial incentive you must work hard, or you may possibly (or likely) lose your money. But the buzz is that you also have the opportunity to earn dramatically more money than as a traditional worker-bee employee. Why not own your hive instead?

The Basics Explained

Franchising is a system to operate a business and/or market a service or product that has proven itself through a variety of similar enterprises. There is no one-size-fits-all definition of franchising since this style of business can come in so many different variations. Just about anything basic, relatively simple, understandable, and therefore teachable can be franchised. Less likely to be executed properly in a franchise scenario are businesses that are more technically complicated, difficult to attract workers to, and narrow in sales attraction. So the old KISS formula still applies: keep it simple, stupid.

This form of enterprise begins with a franchise agreement

or license, giving a person, or a group of people (known as the franchisee), the legal right to market a service or product under the name or trademark of the franchisor, utilizing that franchisor's experience and knowhow. Under the contractual terms, training and ongoing support are provided. This is usually down to the smallest detail, from the inception of the decision to start the new business to its opening and thereafter with day-to-day advice.

As a result, some degree of your control of your new business is reduced, but that's something that franchisors also like to jokingly describe as eliminating the right to mismanage your business. In exchange, you pay fees and charges for the transfer of knowledge and services, such as an initial franchise fee and ongoing royalty on sales or other measurements to generate fees to the franchisor for its contribution to your success. Such fees, or a portion thereof, are frequently imbedded in the real estate rent in those franchises where the franchisor provides the location to you.

There is typically a marketing and advertising fee, but your business will get that back directly "in spades" in the promotional effort. For example, as a Dunkin' Donuts franchisee, you will pay a marketing fee, but your fee will be combined with all the other fees from all the shops, and every operation will receive the benefit of all the advertising done to promote the brand. This result isn't so great when there are just a few franchises and a small budget, but then fees overall are usually smaller. Some franchisees complain not only about the fees but the type of advertising itself, as if everyone can be pleased with every word, and some even accuse the franchisor of using the advertising budget to attract new franchisees. Creating interest in the franchise itself may result from all the promotion, but it's usually not the objective.

A shortcut to a successful business at a reasonable cost, the franchise model is the fast track, and perhaps the best route, to marketplace triumph. There is no need to reinvent the wheel and make mistake after mistake. Instead, you, as the franchisee, learn from others who blazed the trail prior to you. This collaborative approach increases your likelihood for success, avoiding the typical newbie errors simply by purchasing the rights to use the franchisor's proven, already successful business model and recognized brand name. Think of it as a demonstrated risk-reduction system designed for a new business to hit the ground running.

This system of virtually cloning a business across a regional or national network usually includes a huge array of diversified essential services provided to establish the new franchise, executed by experienced executives who've performed the services for which they're responsible countless times. This includes:

- Training
- Legal
- Architectural design
- Location analysis
- Negotiation
- Acquisition
- Equipment and fixture selection
- Construction supervision
- Marketing and financing assistance
- Product creation
- Purchase and development
- Everything needed to start, open, and operate your business, including financial control systems

This system provides superlative business management expertise and extensive financial resources, direction, and assistance that probably could not be obtained otherwise—except at huge costs. Combining this with the motivation of a franchisee's financial commitment and practical experience and presence, you create a maximum opportunity for success.

Banks, other financial institutions, and the US Small Business Association all recognize these advantages and their intrinsic value. They are especially aware that the franchisees have their cash invested and are working personally to build equity in their own businesses and are able to sell their franchises in the future for the value that has built up.

Advantages of Franchising

Of the numerous advantages to franchising, perhaps none is more important than creating a safety net of expertise and experience. Seasoned, veteran franchisors offer a great deal of expertise, including:

- **A Formula for Success:** The key to franchising is a proven operating system, which can be easily duplicated across many different territories, often worldwide with minor adjustments. For example, because of the exorbitant cost of rent in Japan, Mister Donut needed to rent ever-smaller spaces, utilizing smaller equipment and fixtures. One twenty-four-inch fryer replaced the typical two thirty-six-inch fryers in each store, and smaller display and counter space was also required. Who would have dreamed of a transfer of expertise and knowhow and recognition a half century ago, when few knew the names of McDonald's, KFC, Hertz, Manpower, Avis, H and R Block, Holiday Inn, or Mister Donut?

- **Location Analysis, Financial and Development Aid:** For those franchises requiring unique locations, like many restaurants or other drive-in type operations, to create a successful enterprise, real estate location analysis, selection, and lease negotiation expertise is tantamount and expertly provided. Decisions are based on actual, innumerable experiences.

  One example is analyzing traffic of proposed locations, which is one of the most important factors for your business. Ask a broker what the traffic count is, and, more frequently than not, the answer will just be, "Great!" That answer is wholly inadequate. A franchisor will become upset with this simplistic response, which is both misleading and uninformative. I used to answer such comments with as shallow a statement as, "I hear the traffic is mostly trucks traveling over sixty-five miler per hour."

  The question is what comprises the traffic, its speed, what percent is trucks, how many women in cars, position of traffic lights, turnarounds, visibility to the site, and a myriad of other factors. In the same way, architects, engineers, and designers work inside and out to construct the spaces for maximum appeal and proven efficiency at minimum expense. As a business ages, they are brought in again to redesign and update. Equipment and fixtures, business software for computers, literally everything down to award lapel pins are selected and purchased based on value and need for operations. The strength of the chain's purchasing power assures fair if not lower

pricing and costs, and the financial stability of the organization also helps provide the opportunity to obtain the best financing from lenders.
- **Research:** Franchisors take selling, serving, or providing a new product or service very seriously and will do so only after conducting exhaustive market research—utilizing both in-house and outside resources. They need your new operation to succeed just as much as you do. Franchisors are ever protective that one rotten apple doesn't spoil the whole barrel. This may have been more important when the chains were very small, but larger operations are devastated by failure, which they take as their own failure.
- **Training:** Those who have walked this lonesome road before offer the freshman class an opportunity to learn everything they need to know about launching and running a successful operation. The knowledge and experience of past successes and failures is yours, delivered on a silver platter. Just as basic training does not make a soldier out of a civilian, training alone for weeks, or months in many cases, does not make an owner a success. But once graduated from learning the basics of how to run your franchise successfully, owners thereafter typically receive follow-up training and regular advice on their operations for the life of the business, with the franchisor keeping a steady eye on results. As franchisees gain ever more experience and work, their management becomes more rote, and sometimes they feel irritated by what may seem like a big brother approach. However, most see the value and appreciate the initiatives and advice. After all, it's for the good of everyone.

- **Brand Name Power:** It's hard to put a price tag on something as valuable as the instant name recognition of top brands, but keep in mind that the better the trademarked name, the higher the cost of the franchise. Priceless ingredients in the recipe for brand recognition may include positive reaction, familiarity, reliability, and confidence from potential customers. Had a Coke lately? Yes, bottlers are franchised too.
- **Advertising, Marketing, and Public Relations:** This is an important part of creating brand name attraction, and franchises provide a built-in promotional source through a variety of forms of public relations contacts, from old-school PR efforts to print and broadcast advertising, as well as modern web and smart phone applications. There's essentially no media that can be ignored in today's world. No individual operator could possibly afford to mount the type of perpetual campaigns that franchisors do, paid for essentially with the marketing and advertising fees collected, as well as in-house contributions. This grows as the company grows, but unfortunately it takes time.
- **Technology Updates:** Specially designed, state-of-the-art technological tools and software designed to maximize sales, analysis, and controls are crucial to keeping even the most basic types of franchise competitive.
- **Purchasing Power:** Bigger businesses obviously purchase in larger quantities, and that means lower prices for the franchisee than any small business owner could ever negotiate. Central purchasing strength provides a greater opportunity

to not only save but to provide higher-quality service and uniformity of product and research and development. Everything from the ingredients used for manufacturing a product to the insurance required to run an operation is likely to be purchased less expensively. Some vendors do not deal with small businesses. Franchisees even have area and regional not-for-profit buying cooperatives to assist in getting the best bang for the buck.

Unlike in the formative years, franchisors have, by law, given up their product profit and replaced it with a higher royalty level or other income source. The same goes for local advertising, now usually administered by the local franchisees through their local co-ops. National advertising is still the domain of the franchisor utilizing some or all of the advertising fee paid by franchisees.

- **Quality Control:** A research and development department provides new and improved systems of operation, as well as ever-evolving product research.
- **Family of Support:** Networking with peers at local, regional, and national conferences organized by franchisors develops ideas and programs to initiate and solve problems. The collective knowledge of the larger group can have a winning and meaningful impact on the individual franchise owners.
- **Future Growth:** With proven success, there is often an opportunity to move ahead and own more than one franchise. In fact, once there is a track record of achievement, a franchisee who wants

to expand will be encouraged to grow. Adding additional franchises has created a huge number of millionaires, and you could become one too.

Disadvantages Discussed

The franchise world is not all wine and roses, of course, but the pros significantly outweigh the cons.

It is important to remember that a franchise is not a license to print money or magically solve all problems inherent in starting a new business. Considerable risk and long-term hard work is required. The biggest drawback is the level of commitment of time, energy, and availability necessary. There is no such thing as partial commitment, or the business will likely not succeed. If you are not present, your presence is not felt, and therefore you could be on the road to failure. The business must even come before family, within obvious limits.

The bigger the business, the greater the desire to build, and the more you are committed to the problems of growth, the more likely you will have a positive result. Big results require a lot of luck, but luck requires a big commitment.

Nobody gets something for nothing, and franchisors are businessmen, first and foremost. They are therefore obligated to turn a profit from their enterprises. Their earnings derive from taking a percentage of each franchise's gross sales, the initial franchise fee, real estate fees, a periodic fee for services, and a fee for financing equipment and improving the property. These services would be significantly more expensive in most cases if venturing out independently. All such services are not available from one source on the open market.

The total of all fees from every source is approximately 10 percent of revenue.

What Is the Potential Downside?

- **Standardization:** You must be willing to follow the franchisor's rules and regulations, which requires a willingness to dispense with your own ego, but none of your efforts, to walk down their proven path to success. There are rules to this game, and you must be willing to play by them to maximize the business.

    Relinquishing control to a consistent standardized business model means you are not actually being a total entrepreneur, at least not in the traditional sense. Entrepreneur and franchisee are in reality worlds apart. The franchisee brings different attributes into play, often with less confidence and experience, and is willing to pay the price to get the necessary guidance for maximizing the chance of success. A franchisee implements somebody else's vision, or concept, that already has a proven track record. The trailblazer who developed the original model to be implemented is actually the entrepreneur, for whatever benefit that brings.

    There is much to be gained from relinquishing this control, but you must be willing and able to conform to the multitude of preordained standards, requirements, and procedures. Franchisees are restricted by the rules and regulations of their contracts. This is not a negative tradeoff for most and actually protects the average small business owners from themselves, their own costly errors, and those of their fellow franchisees.

    If this concept terribly disappoints you or is

not the nature of your personality down to your very core then stop here. Do not pass go; do not collect two hundred dollars (with apologies to the makers of Monopoly). Even if you think you've found a better way to accomplish things along the way, it is still a big no-no to make such changes. For example, you can never choose to carry a less expensive brand of cola, or even a different brand, than the franchisor commands. There are likely to be national contracts with bottlers requiring all stores to purchase the same soda product in order to secure the pricing, free equipment, and signs. One frequent issue between franchisees and their home office is over advertising type, degree, and content—but guess who always wins.

Nowhere is the domination of the big corporation more in evidence than the detailed operations manual handed down to new franchisees. This is your bible. Worship it. Everything is detailed in terms of running the operation, from pricing to customer service, inventory and hours.

- **Cost to the Franchisee:** Then, of course, there's the issue of money—yours…and often a great deal of it. Another company is using your capital to get their product to market rather than build their own company-owned stores. Therefore it is not necessary for them to take out a loan to build another location. You, on the other hand, will be required to dig deep into your pockets and/or come to terms with lending institutions. In addition, after paying an initial franchise fee, there are usually the aforementioned ongoing royalties, advertising, and real estate fees.

The franchisor earns incrementally on each franchise and garnishes the lion's share of the profits. The franchisee has most of the financial risk, however. It is costly for the franchisor to open a franchise, and it will be very damaging to the franchisor's reputation if it fails. Even so, the substantial financial loss remains with the franchisee if there is a failure.
- **Growth Potential Limitations:** The success of the franchise can lead to explosive growth potential, with the opportunity of opening many more similar franchises. Such potential could also be restricted for a variety of reasons. For instance, if other geographic regions nearby are already taken, there could possibly be no room left for growth in the area, and your success could not be built on, except in possibly a new area, losing the benefit of nearby staff support.
- **Hand-Me-Down Problems:** Errors and situations created by others that you have no control over can quickly become your problems as well. The franchisors could make business and public relations blunders that could not only hurt their businesses but yours as well. Litigation and tax problems can snowball into full-blown catastrophes for the name and reputation of your hard-earned piece of the pie since the franchisee's success is directly tied to the franchise as a whole. Unforeseen problems or other franchisees' lack of success can easily result in a faltering image for all subsidiaries.

For example, in the Yves St. Laurent operation, Mr. St. Laurent died, and that resulted in the

demand for his designs all but disappearing. Therefore, all of the YSL boutiques were forced to close their doors since there was no more product to sell.
- **Term Limitations:** The original franchise agreement's duration can be set by the main branch, making for a more expensive future. Getting in early is the only answer, but the earlier you get in, the less knowledge the franchisor has and the less well-known the brand. All these issues need to be evaluated by you in making your choice.
- **Power and Control:** Although professional advice from a franchisor is designed to create a success, this can also at times be seen to be creatively restrictive. This is the cross that management bears since such limits must be set by someone to prevent business anarchy. The big brother corporation assists the little brother with quality control, service and even cleanliness, and controls through inspection reports, while providing significant advice on all related business matters. There is still enough leeway for management to operate, but the contract's discipline also prevents many potential missteps and mistakes.

There is only room for one lion in this jungle, and the nature of the beast is that power rests primarily with the corporation. The ultimate recourse for any contractual obligation is the ability to cancel the franchise, but it is seldom exercised in the real world since persuasion usually works better than force.

The Brand and Beyond

The franchise's good name and image, also known as brand, is perhaps the single most important thing they bring to the table. The reputation of their name is how people perceive their products or services and is what a franchisee is really seeking to purchase when going into business. Most customers don't know or care who owns the individual stores or restaurants and are walking through the doors strictly on the basis of name recognition. A customer knows what to expect after seeing the familiar logo before entering. The brand represents a promise to the customer that each franchise must keep.

A variety of elements combines to create the contemporary brand, including products, values, tradition, design, personality, graphics, and advertising. Simply mentioning those iconic golden arches or viewing the McDonald's logo conjures up very specific images, including types of products, décor, and even a virtual taste experience. A lot of effort and substantial sums of money have been spent to create this response.

All of the top franchises immediately summon very detailed images to the consumer's mind. Picture the snapshot that pops up in your head when the following other top brands are mentioned: Burger King, Domino's Pizza, Panera Bread, 7-Eleven, Edible Arrangements, and Jiffy Lube. I bet some of the fast food restaurants even made you salivate more than Pavlov's dog! This illustrates the fundamental principles of dynamic brand awareness, such as "You deserve a break today," "Time to make the donuts," "Have it your way," and "We try harder."

At their best, some brands drive passionate devotion among their followers. "Think different" was the slogan that brought Apple to prominence, and they truly did follow their theme. The release of the company's products draws long lines to their stores and brings an almost religious-like fervor among legions of rabid fans. Sight unseen, a new iPhone release is greeted with the same level of buzz and anticipation as a new Beatles album was in the 1960s.

This is behind the concept of what a franchisee is expecting to purchase by entering into an agreement with a big-name corporation. That's why larger and more famous brands are able to charge so much more for a franchise, since they are bringing increased name recognition. The goal of the initial franchise fee is to cover the company's cost of training and opening a new location. Thereafter, the rent/real estate markup and/or royalty on sales serve as their profit centers. Today, product purchasing is in the hands of the franchisee, subject to product guidelines, and the franchisor usually does not profit off of it. However, secret products like Coca Cola need never disclose their formula, and profit is built into the sale price.

The brand name is a strategic partnership that offers the customer's trust, confidence, and integrity. The less brand awareness in a new market, the more time, energy, and advertising dollars required. Remember, though, the flip side of the coin is that if that brand name is significantly tarnished, all of the individual affiliates suffer as well.

2

The History of Franchising

The beginnings of franchising can be traced back as far as the Middle Ages, when Catholic Church created franchise-style contracts with tax collectors for a percentage of money they collected for the Church. Although this practice ended by the late 1500s, English franchises for fairs, markets, and ferries were granted in the seventeenth century. The licensees were required to pay a fee (called a "royalty") to the royal treasury after each collection in exchange for protection.

In those days it would have been impossible to imagine that franchising would one day evolve into the modern billion-dollar global industry of today. The system has grown rapidly into a wide variety of types of businesses, including food, retail, automotive, personal service, and business service. There are about eighty-five subcategories—from fast food (McDonald's, Wendy's, ad nauseum) to real estate (Coldwell Banker, RE/MAX) and lodging (Embassy Suites, AmeriSuties). Other examples include homes and business damage restoration (ServPro), and even dog walking services and a soccer school for toddlers. There are now over a million franchise units operating in the United States alone.

In the Beginning…

The origin of the word "franchising" comes from the French word "franc," translated as "freedom" or "liberty." Peasants or serfs were granted certain rights, such as hunting, or certain types of businesses by landowners during the Middle Ages (the fifth through fifteenth centuries)—a far cry from today's McDonald's.

In the nineteenth century, German and British breweries granted rights to local pub owners to distribute their products. Since these franchisees were in a terrible financial situation, the breweries offered money in exchange for being the exclusive brand sold in a pub, even if prices were increased.

The birth of American franchising is commonly attributed to sewing machine inventor Isaac Merritt Singer (1811–1875). The Singer Sewing Machine Company founder created a technological breakthrough for housewives accustomed to sewing everything by hand. The machines, however, cost a whopping $125 each, a price tag that many could not afford in those days. A $1.15-a-day installment plan was developed to solve the problem, but most people were still intimidated by the first commercial sewing machines.

Singer created the American franchising model in 1851, when he began soliciting dealer agents nationwide to exclusively sell his sewing machines in exchange for a small licensing fee. They also trained customers to use the machines as a way of helping them over the hurdle of being intimidated by the new technology. The concept was such a major success that the company's sales skyrocketed 80 percent by 1860.

Hair care expert Martha Matilda Harper was another early franchise innovator, advocating the use of organic chemicals in shampoos and, in the late 1800s, launching one of the most successful hairdressing franchise systems in the country. Working as a domestic servant in Rochester, New York, Harper saved her money to open her own salon and shampoo manufacturing business. She began by using her own luxuriously long head of hair to market her products and services. Demand surged through word of mouth, and in 1891 she opened her first franchise outlet in Buffalo, New York.

Harper broke new ground not just in business but as an early feminist by training disenfranchised women to become successful entrepreneurs. Much like Harper, they were former domestic servants struggling to make ends meet with their meager salaries. These women trained in her beauty schools located in places such as Rochester, New York, and Atlanta, Georgia, and as far north as Harper's native Alberta, Canada. Following graduation, these women were franchised different territories for their business. At the company's peak, there were over five hundred franchised outlets, serving influential clients such as President Woodrow Wilson and Jackie Kennedy.

Another entrepreneur commonly referred to as one of the godfathers of modern franchising is David Liggett. He formed a "drug cooperative" in 1902 with about forty druggists to create private-label products in their own manufacturing company. Business boomed under their new name, Rexall, and they franchised their merchandise to a growing number of enthusiastic pharmacists. This became a blueprint for many other franchisors that soon followed in their footsteps.

At the turn of the century, the United States was caught up in the industrial revolution, and automobile franchises came of age. Car dealerships' franchising roots began growing under Detroit, Michigan, car salesman William Metzger. After selling his stake in a bicycle shop, the automotive enthusiast built one of the first automobile dealerships in the United States. The concept began with the electric-powered Waverly in 1897, and then more brands followed, such as Oldsmobile, General Motors, and Cadillac.

Entrepreneur H.O. Kohller jumped on the bandwagon, selling Winton automobiles, manufactured by Cleveland-based Winton Motor Carriage Company in Reading, Pennsylvania. The best remembered of the automotive pioneers, however, was certainly Henry Ford with his Model T line. With his mass-produced cars, Ford needed dealers across the nation to keep up with the demand. His dealer-franchise system was nothing short of an American revolution. Eventually he constructed factories in every country on good terms with the United States, with accompanying dealerships.

Following in the footsteps of Ford was George Pepperdine, a twenty-three-year old Kansas City bookkeeper from the auto parts industry. In 1909, he sold mail order replacement parts, opening a retail store in 1921. The demand for auto parts grew through the years to service Ford's mass-produced vehicles.

Pepperdine grew to a dozen stores and then sold his business to printing salesman Don Davis, who expanded the company by selling franchises. Through this franchising system, which he called "associate store program," his business expanded to four thousand in towns and cities. Pepperdine went on to establish the Christian liberal arts college that would become Pepperdine University.

Much of what became modern franchising comes from a system established by beverage companies, with soft drink businesses selling their specialty syrups to local bottlers instead of selling the actual drink. This proved cheaper because of shipping and transportation limitations.

The Coca-Cola Company entered the franchising marketplaces in 1889 after seeing the distribution advantages. Benjamin

Thomas and Joseph Whitehead from Chattanooga were given exclusive rights to bottle and sell the syrup concentrate that the company produced. Bottlers around the world continue to manufacture over five hundred brands in cans and bottles under the same agreement with the Coca-Cola Company.

A few years later, Pepsi-Cola followed their number-one competitor's lead into the world of franchising. Caleb Davis Bradham expanded his business in 1905, offering franchises to bottlers in Charlotte and Durham in North Carolina. By 1910, the number grew to 250, and the company also modernized its delivery system with the use of motor vehicles.

Postwar Boom

Roy Allen partnered with his former employee Frank Wright to sell their patented root beer in 1922, using their initials, A&W. Their beverage stands were leased to operators in Sacramento. A year later, the first franchised drive-in restaurant was born, and ten years later 170 franchises were successfully operating.

The restaurant and hotel chain Howard Johnsons was another style of franchising. The owner opened his second restaurant in Orleans, Massachusetts, in 1932; four years later, thirty-nine more restaurants opened, and by 1939 there were 170 more. The total was up to 340 by the time the business went public in 1961.

The big franchise boom in America occurred following World War II, beginning slowly in the 1940s and early 1950s. This marked the beginning of business format franchising, a turnkey approach that created the modern-day franchise.

The ultimate franchise success story is found in the shadow of the golden arches. In 1954, Raymond Albert Kroc began his franchising career after working odd jobs, such as driving an ambulance in World War I and selling paper cups, plates, and multi-mixers for milkshakes and frappes. When he visited Dick and Mac McDonald's burger shop in San Bernardino, California, to sell his milkshake mixers, Kroc heard the proverbial opportunity knocking. The assembly line system of quickly preparing food was exceptionally efficient and quick, and the brothers had already begun successfully franchising their business.

The brothers were hesitant about franchising throughout the country, and Kroc seized the opportunity to follow up in the rest of the nation. The McDonald's Corporation offered long-term franchises and by 1959 had grown 63 percent. Kroc paid $2.7 million to the McDonald brothers in 1961 to buy them out. Two years later, it was 84 percent higher, and by 1963 the company built its five hundredth restaurant. Kroc referred to franchising as the "updated version of the American Dream." As of 2013, they were the largest hamburger fast food restaurants in the world, serving sixty-eight million customers daily in 119 countries.

A similar American success story was Colonel Harland Sanders, who in 1930 started his food business career at a Kentucky gas station with the Sanders Court and Café. He introduced a secret fried chicken recipe in 1940, creating a clucking sensation. When a new interstate system left his restaurant stranded from the traffic in 1955, he began marketing his recipe to other area restaurant owners. He received a five-cent royalty fee for every piece of chicken sold, and by 1960 Kentucky Fried Chicken's franchises grew to 190 outlets. Three years later, it had grown 67 percent. The company was purchased by Jack Massey and former Kentucky governor John Brown in 1963 and had grown into a $12-million sensation.

Some of the best-known franchises came of age in the '50s and '60s, including Holiday Inns, Burger King, 7-Eleven, Baskin-Robbins, Roto-Rooter, Dunkin' Donuts, Mister Donut, H&R Block, Lee Myles, Midas Muffler, and Pearle Vision Center.

The legendary Dave Thomas began his own fast food empire running KFC franchises, shining brightly with creative promotional suggestions, such as the iconic red-and-white-striped bucket, the revolving bucket-like sign, and Sanders appearing in his own commercials. He then went on to found his own hamburger restaurants, Wendy's, offering what he felt was an improvement on McDonald's hamburger product. By 1972, he grossed $1.8 million annually with nine outlets. By the end of the decade, he had five thousand outlets across the world. He himself became a household name by starring in his own commercials.

Boston Chicken became a huge success, with thousands of stores nationwide, after Aaron Spencer and George Naddaff sold the Boston-based KFC chain and created Boston Chicken. In fact, thousands of franchise owners became multi-millionaires developing multi-store franchise chains within their parent franchisor chains or through new franchise creations.

The first Dunkin' Donuts, originally The Open Kettle Donut Shop, was christened in 1950 in Quincy, Massachusetts, by William Rosenberg. In 1955, the company's first franchise was opened in Worcester, Massachusetts.

Case Study: Mister Donut

This book is not meant to detail the steps to open a new franchise offering or tell the story of Mister Donut and other franchises I led but to relate some of my experiences so that they can serve as a guide to future franchisees and franchisors. Throughout this book, I reference anecdotes from my own personal experiences, hopefully demonstrating how progress and success were achieved with these new opportunities. Because I regard their businesses greatly, McDonald's, Howard Johnson's, and a few others are mentioned where appropriate as well.

My foray into franchising began with Mister Donut in 1957, while I was a first-year law student. My father-in-law was the brother-in-law, CPA, and eventual partner of Bill Rosenberg in Dunkin' Donuts. They separated several years later as Dunkin' Donuts expanded rapidly, and my father-in-law opened the first Mister Donut Shop in Revere, Massachusetts, in 1955.

While I was in law school, he asked me to join him in Mister Donut, but I wasn't becoming a lawyer to run donut shops. So we discussed franchising the operation, as Dunkin' Donuts was then doing, which, after some investigation and research, seemed like a real opportunity. Franchising was so new on the business scene that few knew much about it. As a future member of the bar, which I was determined to become first, I would at least have some anti-trust, contracts, real estate, and legal training that most others did not. We made a deal to be equal partners in future shops that would be franchised, and, upon becoming a member of the Massachusetts Bar, I started franchising Mister Donut Shops full time.

This became the business future of Mister Donut, and our subsequent franchise agreement, cobbled together from many others being used then—along with my editing and input—became the substance for other franchisors. The franchising concept itself was unique, and franchising usually limited their exposure to others. McDonald's and Howard Johnson's were the best-known franchisors then and set the example for many to follow and build upon.

Howard Johnson's franchise contract, specifically the provisions pertaining to the exclusive purchasing of food products solely from Howard Johnson's, was eventually thought to be unlawful for operations whose products were really not proprietary. Therefore, requiring purchasing of all products, instead of merely setting standards for non-secret products, like cups and boxes, put all franchisors in serious jeopardy of violating federal law regarding exclusive dealing requirements. This legal issue put Chicken Delight out of business, closing one thousand stores.

With a burgeoning industry, a group of successful franchisors formed the International Franchise Association in 1959 at a Chicago Franchise, Start Your Own Business Show. I was one of that pioneering group and served as an initial director and head of the legal committee. Our objective was to create a group to maintain a favorable commercial and regulatory atmosphere for franchising. The organization continues to serve as a watchdog group and keeps the industry respectable, offering extensive, high-quality educational programs for franchisors and franchisees.

The IFA's initial goal was to elevate the reputation of franchising, which suffered from the sale of questionable and some illegal "opportunities." There were only about twenty-five members at its introduction, and for the first few years the organization suffered from its members and leaders using it to help sell their franchises, instead of educating franchisors. At that time, no franchisees were allowed to join or attend.

As a founding director, I became the first chairperson of the IFA Legal Committee. Our initial goal was to clean up franchise agreements, many of which at the time might have contained certain unlawful provisions, especially exclusive dealing provisions and similar FTC and Sherman Act violations.

As a director, I had the opportunity to meet several top New York City anti-trust lawyers, including Gerald Van Cise of the law firm Cahill Gordon Reindel and Olme, and the then extremely well-regarded head of the US Federal Trade Commission, Mary Gardiner Jones. These experiences educated me about reducing and even eliminating franchise restrictions considerably.

The principal question that needed to be considered was: are your restrictions really necessary? And any that weren't, or that a franchisor could do without, were struck from franchise agreements. This at least made them seem more reasonable and fair.

As a result, I founded a new educational opportunity for franchising at Boston College, my law school alma mater, named The Boston College Center for the Study of Franchising. It was highly attended by executives and even suppliers and was a significant success, bringing in a large membership, and leading the way to more franchise information and idea exchange experiences.

Business Week magazine did a major article as a result of the size and quality of the first Boston College Franchise Conference, entitled "Franchising Finds It's an Industry." I also taught an adult education course on franchising in the Boston College Business School, which was well attended.

In addition, a summer program was developed with the US Department of Labor, wherein high school dropouts (nongraduates over age eighteen) were hired into franchise training programs. The federal government paid half of their minimum-wage salaries. On completion of training, they were awarded a graduation certificate signed by the vice president of the United States, Hubert Humphrey, and then the majority kept being employed by the franchise. They were encouraged to graduate from high school, and the goal was for their training to earn them more than minimum wage in the future. Hundreds participated in the program, which ran successfully for two years.

In 1963, I was very fortunate to be able to join the Young Presidents Organization, a worldwide educational group for CEOs of businesses with over one hundred employees and annual revenues of more than $10 million. There were fewer than one thousand members then, but today there are over ten thousand. At age fifty, YPOers transition into the World President's Organization, which now has fifteen thousand members. Both organizations run local, regional, area, and world meetings and seminars, and members have access to world-class resources, such as speakers and presenters. World leaders in every field have been our guests.

I even received an honorary doctor of law degree from the New England School of Law in Boston. The main speaker and another recipient that graduation day was former ABC *Nightline* host Ted Koppel, who delivered the graduation speech. The other recipients were distinguished state and federal judges.

The Psychedelic '60s and Day-Glo '70s

The first meaningful book on franchising, *The Franchise Boom, How You Can Profit From It*, was written by Harry Kursh in 1962, when Mister Donut had just a handful of stores. It was very well received, and it helped promote the industry. I was interviewed for the book at the New York Coliseum during the first Start Your Own Business show. Mister Donut had a booth, and since I was a member of the Massachusetts Bar, I was asked to give a lecture on franchise agreements and the law. Harry Kursh attended my presentation, which resulted in Mister Donut being prominently featured from the very first page of the book.

I was honored as an Outstanding Young Man of Boston by the Greater Boston Chamber of Commerce in 1964. Prior honorees included John Glenn and Ted Kennedy, among other notable local figures. The award recognized my involvement as a leader in the growing franchising industry due to the growth of Mister Donut, creating their college Franchise Center and Business Exposition, editing three books on franchising, community philanthropic work, and leadership in the worldwide Young Presidents Organization.

In the mid-1960s, franchise activity kicked into high gear. Food franchising success story Fred DeLuca was a seventeen-year-old high school graduate who partnered with his friend Dr. Peter Buck in 1965 to open a Bridgeport, Connecticut, sandwich restaurant. With only $1,000 in capital to start off, they built their business into a franchise empire called Subway. They went on to become the second-largest worldwide restaurant operator.

By the end of the psychedelic 1960s, there were over one hundred thousand new franchise units in the United States alone. Some people took advantage of this new trend and damaged their good reputations in the process, such as brothers John Jay and Henry Hooker. The Nashville family sold shares of stock for Minnie Pearl's Fried Chicken to various influential investors, only opening a handful of franchise outlets by 1968, according to press reports.

Their complete lack of restaurant and business experience led to their reporting, as others also did as it was then an accepted accounting practice, entire initial franchise fees for large territories, with only a very small percent of that fee paid down as income. For example, a $100,000 fee with only a portion of that fee paid down would be reported as $100,000 of income before any store-opening performance was accomplished. This helped result in their downfall and the closing of what was reported as a large percentage of their stores by 1970. It also led to a virtual gold rush of celebrity franchise imitators utilizing the names of celebrities such as Tex Ritter, Tennessee Ernie Ford, and Mickey Mantle, who, like so many franchisors, attended Boston College Franchise Center events.

The US Securities and Exchange Commission officially investigated the Minnie Pearl situation, their stock plummeted, and the State of California legislated the first franchise sales laws. Other states followed in the years to come, and in 1978, the Federal Trade Commission mandated franchisors to provide to any prospect, within ten days of their first meeting and before any cash is paid down, a Uniform Franchise Offering Circular (UFOC). In 2007, this regulation document was updated and renamed the Franchise Disclosure Document (FDD).

Over half of all franchises were gas stations in 1970, but due to the Arab oil embargo and gasoline shortages, almost thirty-two thousand stations closed between 1973 and 1976.

Both Mister Donut and Dunkin' Donuts had over one hundred locations by 1963. In the 1980s, Allied Domeque (NYSE) purchased Dunkin', and by the late 1990s, their two thousandth store was opened. International Multifoods, the world's largest flour producers, purchased Mister Donut in 1969 and sold it in the late '80s to Allied Domeque, which merged about half of the more than fifteen hundred noncompeting Mister Donut shop locations with Dunkin'. Dunkin' Donuts Brands Group issued its IPO in July 2011, and shares quickly shot up 46 percent. They now have some fifteen thousand stores worldwide.

There is one significant new twist regarding more recent donut shop expansion. Until just a few years ago, nearly all donut shops hand-cut their own donuts in their own kitchens.

There were satellite operations as well, like a counter in a discount house, but recently a commissary system has been introduced. The donuts today are made centrally, primarily by machine, and then delivered to each shop. Thereafter shops could be opened in smaller, secondary locales, like in a gas station or convenience store, and if a minimum, adequate volume isn't reached, it could be moved at little cost.

By this time, stores were all over the world. Mister Donut was the first to expand to Canada, where it had operations in Ontario and Quebec. We helped celebrate the five hundredth Mister Donut opening in Tokyo, Japan, where Mister Donut is significantly dominant. Franchise development rights as well as the name Mister Donut were sold to a Japanese conglomerate, and except for the name "Mister Donut" and an official ribbon-cutting, there is no contact.

A franchising believer to the core, I acquired, in 1969, ABC Mobile Brake, a California-based automotive aftermarket franchise that I expanded from just a couple of franchises into a couple of hundred, operating in all fifty states. I founded the fast food delicatessen Sizzleboard, with some four hundred franchises sold between 1970 and 1974, but sold it all off when it was determined that the five-sandwich menu was too narrow, and expanding it into a sandwich and hamburger operation was not what we wanted to develop because there were so many hamburger stores, but likely we should have.

1980s to 1990s

Franchising continued going strong into the 1980s, with more than 356,000 franchised businesses, up from the eighteen thousand of 1973. Sales reached a whopping $474 billion by the middle of the decade, with the US Department of Commerce estimating franchising to account for 34 percent of all retail sales in America.

One of the biggest success stories of the era was Wendy's renewed popularity explosion, with the iconic "Where's the Beef?" campaign becoming a national catchphrase in 1984.

About sixteen hundred businesses were franchised in the 1980s, and by the end of the next decade the amount had tripled and beyond. One particularly hot item in the '80s was frozen yogurt, currently experiencing a big comeback after being displaced by specialty ice cream shops in the 1990s. Over 50 percent of all retail sales in America in the late '90s were by franchises, with about $1 trillion in sales, the IFA reported.

The international market for American franchisors was also rapidly expanding during the '80s, reaching as far as Russia and South Africa. This continued in the 1990s with foreign franchisors, such as the London-based The Body Shop, entering the American market, which led to the boom in food, retail, and service industries.

In my own franchising world, I continued opening new concepts and founded Omnidentix in 1982, revolutionizing dental services with the first chain of walk-in, high-retail foot traffic and shopping mall dental centers operating along the East Coast. Omnidentix succeeded in the face of very strong opposition from state dental boards. As soon as we advertised an opening date of a dental center, the local dental board, claiming illegal advertising, threatened to revoke our dentists' licenses, making them panic. Advertising by professionals, doctors, dentists, and lawyers was made legal by the US Supreme Court's decision in the Bates case.

A major hearing was held by the Massachusetts Dental Board, fully covered by the press. Legal briefs were submitted by a constitutional law professor and a top trial lawyer as was a letter from the Massachusetts attorney general to the dental board, stating that dentists could now legally advertise. An African MIT student testified that without his being able to go to Omnidentix, where prices were low and availability maximized, he would not have been able to afford the dental care he needed.

The dental board withdrew its objection, and when we faced this kind of opposition again, we were able to merely send copies of the hearing and the briefs, letters, testimony, and result. Soon the threats to cancel dentists' licenses stopped. Today, dental centers and medical clinics are everywhere, and ads by lawyers fill the yellow pages of telephones books. As I frequently lectured, our population was underserved by dentists. Fifty percent of the population had no dentist, and Omnidentix only expected to serve this market.

Next was Mobile Muffler in 1985, similar to Mobil Brake but servicing automotive exhaust systems. Although successful business-wise, Mobile Automotive operators preferred brake repair because of the discomfort of having to service mufflers under the car, which was more strenuous on the body and neck.

The Mobile operations were followed by Smartel, an originator of prepaid promotional telephone cards, which was sold to AT&T. Finally, Americounsel (Internet legal-forms provider in multiple languages) was launched, which was similar to but predating Legal Zoom. Unfortunately, this was just as the high-tech boom went bust—and with it the last $1 million of $10 million of our venture capital funding. Capital was committed but yet to be received. Every time I see a Legal Zoom advertisement today, I imagine our multilanguage, multidisciplinary computer programs written for us in each area of the law by the chair of that legal area in the American Bar Association.

Franchising Today

It is amazing that today franchising represents an estimated $472 billion, according to the IFA. Franchising is the fastest-growing type of small business, according to the US Small Business Administration, generating eight to fourteen new jobs with each new franchise. That translates to three hundred thousand new jobs annually, with a new business opening every eight minutes each business day.

The top ten franchises for 2013, according to *Entrepreneur* magazine, are, in descending order: Hampton Hotels, Subway, Jiffy Lube, 7-Eleven, Supercuts, Anytime Fitness, Servpro, Denny's, McDonald's, and Pizza Hut. Some of the hottest franchises today include fitness centers, organic health products and services, resale outlets, spa and health services, child care services, and fast food restaurants.

The international franchise market continues to grow, first with Canada, where we were the first to open in Toronto, proving very lucrative for American-based businesses. International borders seemed to melt away with successful American businesses invading such diverse countries as Russia, Saudi Arabia, and Japan.

China now has the most franchises, among them Mister Donut (owned by the Japanese franchise), of any country. As in the United States, I expect Asia to grow to giant operations, and it makes sense. Start a business for yourself but not by yourself. In areas where underemployment is enormous and the need for jobs is huge, coupled with a formidable work effort, franchising will successfully explode.

Franchising has indeed come a long way since the Middle Ages!

3

A Potpourri

When most people hear the word "franchise," they probably think of a teenager in a paper hat asking, "Do you want fries with that?" But the wonderful world of franchising is not just about fast food. The opportunities are multiplying and evolving annually, and today there are literally hundreds of different types of businesses to choose from. It seems like franchisors are only limited by their own creativity.

Franchising in not a synonym for "hamburger." It is instead a systematic approach to distribution. In fact, restaurants only represent approximately a third of what's currently available. Some of the most popular franchises may surprise you since they involve no deep fryer at all. They include businesses as diversified as the UPS Store, Super 8 Motel, Curves for Women, and Matco Tools. Automotive, building, remediation, and senior and child care are all the rage today and among the most popular businesses. A lengthy list of categories can be found at www.franchise.org. Many can be further broken down into subcategories offering a variety of different services. The myriad opportunities can be overwhelming but relax and enjoy the exploration until something rings a bell in your head.

An appropriate way to get started making a selection would be based on your own interests and available capital, but no matter what you chose, remember that you must follow the golden rule of working super hard. You can also study what's hot and what's not, but be careful chasing such business trends since what was popular last year may not be as much in demand this year—and the oldies just grow larger. The bigger picture, such as Americans trending toward wanting to make healthier food choices, could have a dramatic impact on your bottom line if you're selling only deep fried foods, but older franchisors are aware of this and have diversified their menus, and new franchisors also steer clear of one-act offerings. Also keep an eye on the fast-changing technological breakthroughs that can dramatically affect an industry. Such disruptive forces can wipe out entire industries virtually overnight. The Model T savaged the horse and buggy whip industry, as did computers for the typewriter business.

Types of Franchises

Think of the opportunities in three investment categories. The least costly are those businesses that can be operated from home. These usually require about fifty thousand dollars in capital, including the initial franchise fee and working capital, which would be necessary to cover your lack of other income during the startup phase (if necessary, and likely). The next level contains smaller operations that have gross revenues likely under $1 million per year, which usually require investing $250,000 to $350,000 initially. The larger operations start with investments of a minimum of $500,000, such as larger restaurants.

The two most common forms of franchising are business format and product distribution, with the difference depending primarily on what is being manufactured.

Product distribution arrangements are those of a supplier

and dealer, where the franchisee sells the franchisor's products in a supplier-dealer arrangement. Soft drink, automotive, and gasoline industries are usually handled this way, where a trademark and logo is supplied but not an entire business system. Coca-Cola bottlers would be a successful, long-running example of this style. With this model you'll get the building and equipment plans, as well as the operations manuals, but construction, furnishings, fixtures, and equipment are all up to you.

Business format franchises are the most common form and also include the entire system for franchisees to conduct their business, including real estate location, fixtures, opening, operations, and marketing specifics. There is a laundry list of examples of this type, from McDonald's to Midas. The franchisor's operating and procedures manuals are very detailed and specific for these types of enterprises, ensuring proven minimum quality and standards. Consistency is the key with this kind of franchise, and this is why these businesses look nearly identical wherever you find them in the world.

Conversion franchising, a more recent format, is a modification of the typical arrangements discussed above. This example occurs when an independent operator takes on the identity, service, or trademarks of the franchisor. It is like putting a new jacket over a familiar old outfit, without making all the changes business format franchisees would involve. Real-estate brokers and various trade businesses often utilize this.

Franchise arrangements for business owners include single (or direct) unit and multi-unit franchises. As it sounds in the first example, the right to open a single unit is granted by the franchisor. Building an empire, however, requires a multi-unit franchise for area development or to be a master franchise with sub-franchising rights. Of course, singles can often become multis after they have a record of proven success. Indeed, franchisors look to develop from within where possible.

Area development franchises allow the opportunity to open multiple units over a specified period of time in an exclusive territory. A master franchise agreement is even broader than the area contract. In addition to the previously described rights, this type also offers the ability to sell franchises to others, called sub-franchises, taking on many of the responsibilities of the franchisor and sharing with the franchisor the initial franchise fee and continuing royalties and any other profit streams.

A similar relationship is the area representative franchise, where owning a territory offers the opportunity to sell franchises in the area but does not involve day-to-day interaction with the new franchisee, which the franchisor provides after the agreement is made. Although the contract is signed with the franchisor, a portion of original and continuing fees and income streams goes back to the area representative for selling the franchise.

What Makes a Successful Franchise?

Work is the secret sauce for success. Of course, a great concept and building a quality team to create a strong brand and then good old-fashioned hard work are what make a franchise successful. There is no free ride. If you think you can buy a franchise and drive away in a Cadillac, you're naïve or worse.

Franchising is about an initial success, which may mean one, two, ten, or more successful operations and perpetual replication. By the time the product or service is distilled down to the franchisee level, it is simplified—as is frequently described as "idiot-proof"—so that the execution of the staff is almost rote, drilled in, and all but automatic, and everything about it makes sense instinctively. The more the system's plan has been previously executed, the better it becomes. Indeed, the more creative the business is, the more thought required to execute, the more expertise necessary, the less viable the franchise.

Every successful franchise starts with management knowhow. Without good leadership, a business is like a ship without a captain. Dedicated management with "skin in the game," a term frequently used for owners coupled with cash at risk, understand the market viability of the product through research, training, and practical experience and is able to convey that knowledge to staff to properly grow the company. They learn to forecast profits, control cash and limit losses, and constantly follow up new strategies for future successes. The support offered for structuring a new business is invaluable, and they can help guide and budget based on previous experience.

Soak up the knowledge available out there from books such as this, as well as the plethora of websites available. Proper training from the franchisor will bring your business picture into clearer focus and is essential during startup and throughout the initial growth stages. Journalism 101 teaches that the only dumb question is the one you didn't ask, and the same holds true when considering the purchase of a franchise and for dealing with management.

Once you're actually heading into business, your franchisor will help you hire your team to develop and support your success. Take the necessary time and energy to keep learning and constantly lead well through example, following the predetermined program and strategies that are laid out for you.

As you would expect, the franchisor has an experienced and, in most cases, committed and competent team in place with whom you will deal extensively on a regular basis. That, combined with a growing and ever more solid financial base and proven track record for building and growing their business, will help get you off the ground and build a good future. But I can't emphasize enough that your future is up to you, how diligent and committed you are. The franchisor will not run your business. They'll give you the keys and lay the tracks, but you have to be the engineer that drives the train.

Engage your employees as the valuable assets they truly are, treating them with dignity and respect, even as you constantly supervise, teach, train, and manage them and their interactions with others within and outside the company. All are of differing ages, backgrounds, education, ambition, and experiences. But you need them to work in support of each other and the company goals, and they know that too. Frequent employee turnover is a red flag that your selection, training, and leadership are less than what is needed for the situation, and you need help. A happy worker will be more successful at keeping your customers satisfied. All businesses are actually people businesses, and those relationships must be nurtured. Poor people skills take a business down the wrong road and can often lead to failure. If your franchisor or staff members haven't interjected themselves yet and are trying to tip, advise, and guide you to better results, it's likely you're not listening.

Location in businesses where that's a factor is such an essential ingredient in the business stew that a great deal of time clearly must be taken in studying the area, the site, the demographics, the visibility, the sign size limitations, the curb cut requirements, the churches, schools, and type of traffic (i.e., slow, fast, truck, women, men, count, speed). This job needs experts, preferably at the more experienced franchisor level, but at least be certain your target area can sustain your business. You may be selling water in the desert, but if the caravans go on a different route, even you will succumb from thirst.

You can never know your market too well. How many competitors are there in the area, or is that what you want, like auto mile? What's different about your product from others in the same vicinity? There is so much to know and learn about this—let alone the financial deal of the lease, purchase, or whatever the site acquisition method, construction costs and design, zoning, and issues from setbacks to height—that it would take a book exclusively on that subject to lay it all out. But the franchisor can. The real estate brokers may be brilliant; they can help immensely, but they have different motives, which can be deleterious, and they can't know the needs of every operation. No one knows the needs better than the franchisor.

In seeking out a franchise, pick one with a solid base model of multiple operating units, preferably in different markets that have survived through different business cycles. The issue here is not just your goal to seek out a success. The issue is that the most successful usually have the highest fees, cost of entry, and minimal locations available. You'll unlikely, if ever, get a McDonald's franchise in their home town of Chicago, let alone most of the United States, unless it was purchased from an existing franchisee, and the line for that choice is likely long. Make certain there is normally at least an adequate return on investment (ROI) within an appropriate time, after royalties are paid to the franchisor and after you are paid a reasonable manager's salary, if you indeed fill the function of the manager.

Another extremely important issue is starting with enough working capital. This alone often sinks a new business and so will be discussed in great detail in the chapter "Show Me the Money."

Most franchise agreements run a decade, or even multiple decades, in order to justify the investment and provide time for buyers to justify their investments. Therefore try to be as certain as you can that you will be able to work with the people you will inevitably be dealing with.

After your initial success, don't expand too rapidly. Your franchisor will want you to wait until your first franchise is solidly operating before even considering opening another. You must remain attentive to the day-to-day operation of a franchise to win, so keep a laser-like focus on a single unit before even thinking of expanding.

Franchisors must also show a desire to change with the times and invest in growth, such as technological and marketing advances. The franchise relationship is the ultimate in a management incentive and control system. It moves the decision-making process to the lowest common denominator, whose execution is coupled with that special interest of ownership, bringing with it the ability to create equity and potential future capital gain.

Accurate and up-to-date accounting is also essential for the success of a business. I constructed my own guidelines for Mister Donut after I realized I wasn't getting the information I needed in the form I needed it. My ballpark estimates were sometimes closer to reality than some bookkeeping department reports. You must know exactly where you stand financially at all times.

It isn't as easy as just how many franchises are sold and which locations are not yet franchised, or for that matter which franchisees are awaiting locations. These two factors don't necessarily match. You need to be on top of when each store will be ready for equipment, the shipping date, when finance/payment will be arranged, notifying suppliers of the opening date so they can ship inventory and set up credits, the placement of opening promotions and advertisements, and many other date-certain arrangements. We put all that information on a wall display for everyone to check out and act on accordingly, and we distributed an updated weekly printout.

Profitability and Failure Rate

There are always two profits to a successful franchise, one for the franchisor and one for the franchisee. The franchisor makes a little from a lot of franchises, while the franchisee makes all from one (at least before expanding into multiple units). Most franchises work because businesses that are severely flawed never even make it to the next stage of expanding. The business plan should already be a smash hit by the time franchisees are brought aboard—but not all franchises are created equal.

A higher margin of profit can be found with certain products, such as inexpensive dough-based items like bread, pizza, and doughnuts, while meat is much more expensive and sells for more money. Restaurants not requiring real chefs, requiring just cooks or even less skilled food preparers, are less expensive and easier to operate. Before automation, donuts needed a baker who worked quickly with quality but not an expert artisan. Every operation has its required stars, but you need to make everyone a star so that nobody can leave you stranded by unexpectedly leaving. You need to have a pre-thought-out plan in case any such event occurs. If a star like a famous chef is necessary to keep the business afloat, you may have significant trouble on your hands if he or she decides to leave. Perhaps if that individual owned enough equity, that problem could be reduced dramatically.

Almost anything uncomplicated and simply executed can be franchised. It must be packaged and properly, however, and must make sense in cost of investment and availability of personnel.

To check on the overall success of a franchise, learn how many units fail. Item 20 of the Financial Disclosure Document (FDD) must provide a table identifying such failures for the last three years, and contact information is even provided so you can speak to the former franchisee and learn why the unit did not succeed.

The Small Business Administration publishes loan payback failure rates of franchisees. For example, from October 1, 2001, to September 30, 2010, Wings-n-things was listed as the highest percentage of failure, 94.12 percent. Other worst failure rates were Matco Tools, Cold Stone Creamery, Quiznos, and Curves. Among those with zero percent failure were Five Guys Famous Burger and Fries, Hilton Hotels, Piggly Wiggly, Planet Fitness, Ponderosa Steak House, Stanley's Steamer Carpet Cleaning, and Taco Bell.

From the Financial Disclosure Document, a franchise buyer should ideally seek out the profit of a company's average store and compare it to the rate of return on investment of other similar companies' returns. Unfortunately, many companies don't choose to report such information. The methodology that *Forbes* magazine used to select their "Top 20 Franchises for the Buck" included five variables: "average initial investment (franchise fees plus equipment costs); total locations (the more, the better); closure rate (the number of closings in the last three reported fiscal years divided by the total number of existing locations); growth in the number of US outlets in the last three years; and the number of training hours as a percentage of startup cost (the more support from the home office, the better). Overall footprint and survival rates carried the most weight." Using this formula, their top choices included Snap-on, 7-Eleven, and McDonald's.

But life is more than just statistics. It is not a good idea to look at the hottest franchise out there and jump aboard. To determine overall success requires wearing out a little shoe leather and visiting some existing franchisees. They can describe what it's really like to do what they do, the real nitty gritty, day in and day out. If success to you means overall lifestyle of someone running this particular type of business then this is the ideal way to go.

Is Franchising for You?

Franchising is for everybody who is searching for a business opportunity and is willing to work hard, since things do not happen overnight or automatically. This isn't like shoveling coal, so you must have the brains to understand the work as well. On the other hand, Harvard and Wharton MBAs might be the right choice to run a division of a company, or the company itself, but they're not roll-up-their-sleeves-and-get-it-done types. They might be good at running ten stores or one thousand but not at running one, and owning a franchise is a hands-on business that is rote and not very creative or innovative.

But if you just want to kick back, supervise, delegate, and do very little work then no business opportunity is for you. If you don't roll up your sleeves and get some French fry grease on your apron, you are likely not going to succeed. A franchise is created with a solid work ethic and the ability to follow directions from those that came before you to build and perfect the business. Be prepared to work long, hard hours and be sleep deprived. Working capital can be eaten through very quickly, so be prepared.

No matter what the product, business needs can't wait, so you must also be an organized person. Almost all of the most successful franchise owners have similar qualities: they work hard, put business before pleasure, and are very well organized and prepared. First-generation immigrants often have provided the best work ethic for such an environment, but they also often lacked the appropriate funding. The reason this group is so successful at owning franchises may be that they have fewer working options and fewer choice for careers, so they had to make their businesses work—whatever it took.

You may be surprised to learn that I believe that passion is unimportant when running a franchise. After all, there's only so much you can love a donut, for example. But I am certain you will become passionate when you start to see your profits grow.

In reality you are actually buying yourself a job, but it has the potential to make more money than you would be paid as strictly an employee of another person's business. The downside is that you could lose your job and your investment. Although the new business failure rate is much higher for independents than franchises, it is certainly not a universal refuge for the bored, discontented, or unemployed, or anyone who does not have a significant drive to succeed.

Looking into the mirror and honestly analyzing yourself can reveal the answer to the question "Is franchising for you?" Can you manage your own business? You will most likely have to work harder than you ever have before. Are you ready for sixty- to seventy-hour weeks during startup? Can you handle the dirty work if you must do the mopping, trash emptying, firing employees, and handling irate customers? Since you will be interacting with people on a variety of levels, be certain you are a "people person." If not, work on these skills prior to entering the business. Also look inside your own home and study your family. Make sure you have the kind of support network that will be required under stressful conditions and long, hard hours.

If you are still burning with desire to work for yourself then franchising may be the answer to fulfill your dreams. In a world that is becoming increasingly more complex, franchising remains much the same as when I began decades ago—a place where a person's rewards are directly proportionate to his or her labors. This theory leans heavily on Emerson's idea of self-reliance. But due diligence is still required, so do your research since you are making a long-term commitment of time, money, and career.

Opportunities for Young People

As I traveled abroad over the years, I always stopped and asked young people why there seem to be so few of them in some of the non-metropolitan areas I was visiting. I always got the response that industry has shut down, and to get work they had to relocate. The result is that these outlying areas die as young people leave to search for work elsewhere.

Now I find I'm getting a similar response here in the United States. For example, a young waitress from Iowa, a college graduate, recently left her small Iowa town because of a lack of jobs and industry closings. Her sister had relocated to Boston and was working in a restaurant and got her a job there too.

Although fewer jobs may be available as the economy consolidates, you still don't have to leave your hometown (or even your home) to work. You can start your own service, or similar small business, and if possible buy a proven franchise to operate from home. The opportunity is there for you to set out on your own. Rents will be lower in these more economically depressed areas and more employees available at more modest wages. Young people should take the leap while the opportunity is there. Maybe it's not shining directly in your eyes, but it's comforting to know there is such an opportunity.

Franchising Your Business

If you own a business and are seeking a broader expansion, consider developing a franchise division. Expertise is readily available, and you already know the basics and have the expertise in house. In an effort to expand, you might be asking yourself the exact same questions as a franchisee. Once your business has proven itself, it's typical to explore more growth avenues.

But, remember, being a franchisor is also the business of selling businesses to people. That will be new to you, but you can develop the needed skills fairly easily, likely easier than building the business you already did.

Franchising is a system where the product can be changed and the model can remain the same. The techniques and systems that apply to the distribution of one product or service can largely be applied to a very different core business. Once the systems are brought clearly into view, the product or business itself becomes almost incidental.

The first step is proving to yourself that you can do it with a few clones of the operation you plan to franchise and then conduct the necessary market research. Once everything seems in place, that is the time to bring in the experts, such as a franchise attorney and franchise consultant. They can help you develop the necessary franchise disclosure documents, franchise agreement, marketing, real estate, and operations and franchise sales brochures and manuals.

Why should a company consider franchising instead of developing company-owned units? The two prime considerations are how to pay for it and how to manage the operations. The issue of biggest concern is whether local management will be readily available at salaries that fit the model. For example, if highly paid scientists of limited availability are required to manage a science retail store (if there was such a package), that operation should be an in-house company store and not a franchise.

Looking at the international market for expansion can be a winning strategy, but it's best to do it with a local partner with some background and clout. By the time your business is ready to expand globally, hook up with a big-deal partner, as Mister Donut did in Japan. This will be very doable at that point since the franchise is already big, good, and proven. Forget the Mom-and-Pop approach—go big time or don't go at all. After all, what good is one shop in Tokyo?

Starting Your Own Business: A Caveat

In conclusion, I'd like to point out a caveat to the risk of starting your own business. We all need good fortune over what we can't control. The most influential factor that comes to my mind is the economy, availability of capital, and interest rates. If on the day you open your new business there is a serious financial downturn, depending on its depth and length, it is likely to affect you for all the obvious reasons. If your business's working capital reserve is adequate (which, of course, is intertwined with a recession's depth, length, and the speed in which your new customers accept what you're offering), you'll be rewarded with a bridge to safety. If you played it too thinly, with limited and inadequate working capital, you could be in serious trouble.

This, however, shouldn't stop you from entering the wonderful world of franchising. Recoveries follow recessions, and unpredictable things occur all the time. You need to just be aware of the possibilities and plan for them. There could be a product availability issue, or if you opened a drive-in-restaurant it could be a new road construction detour. Hopefully, it's not a complete road change that you missed because you did not do your homework, since this could result in a complete detour of you and your business.

4
Finding a Franchise That Fits Like a Glove

With thousands of different franchises to choose from, it may seem like an extremely daunting task to find the one to which you will dedicate at least a part of your working life. There is no ideal franchise or franchisee, but opportunities, abilities, and interests come in all sizes. The first issue to be determined is what you are interested in. Do you want to clean houses? Can you afford to invest $5 million? Believe me, there is so much out there, you will find something, or probably many things, that you will love. There is really no ideal fit, just utilizing your interests.

To make the best choice, start off by establishing your goals, focusing in on the type of business and lifestyle you are seeking. How hard are you willing and able to work? Some businesses require working nights and weekends (such as convenience stores), while others are more typical nine-to-five weekday systems. If you are uncomfortable supervising larger numbers of employees or working with teenagers then operating a fast food restaurant may not be a good choice for you. Likewise, night owls would not be good choices for donut shops since you will probably be miserable greeting the early morning rush. Finally, how many days a week can you handle working?

Your income requirements are important as well, since

some business will only yield modest dividends no matter how hard you work. Are you seeking to earn a living or make a million dollars?

Take the time to figure out what other commitments you have that will pull you away from your business, such as spouse and children, ailing parents, etc. Now is the time to be realistic before you commit energy or money you can't afford, and all of your good efforts and cash can quickly swirl down the drain.

Fortunately, researching your options utilizing available resources has never been easier. The Internet provides a virtual treasure trove of information, so get comfortable, pour yourself a cup of coffee, and sit back and Google "franchising." You'll find a seemingly infinite universe of material to click on. But be careful; while some of what you find can be valuable expert opinion, much will be fairly useless and could even be completely misleading. One of the best places to begin would be the website of the International Franchise Association (www.franchise.org), whose members are both franchise owners and franchisors and provide a variety of unbiased information and resources. This includes detailed information about over eleven hundred franchises, a list of subject matter experts, and a comprehensive library of franchising information, including legal and regulatory information.

No matter how you begin your quest for knowledge, make sure you understand exactly what a potential franchisor is bringing to the table. If the franchise in question is not offering you broad and significant services then simply forget them. An inexperienced franchisor can be a scary and potentially dangerous partner and can make amateurish mistakes that will affect the franchisee, such as expanding too rapidly, operating too thinly, and even going broke.

If you have a particular interest, that is certainly an excellent place to begin, but ultimately that aspect doesn't really matter.

From my seasoned perspective, donuts or transmissions are essentially the same; they are just another widget to franchise, and so it is really an interest in business that matters first and foremost. Therefore, prospective franchisees should not limit themselves to a specific type of business but should look at how much it costs and having enough money to begin, as well as piggy banking sufficient working capital. There was a time in the wild and wooly early days of franchising when franchisors would take what they could get and run, but those days are long gone, so you better be able to show you're in it for the long haul.

To find a particular franchise that's intriguing to you, research as much as you can about them. A plethora of information will be available online about each and every one, including the all-important complaints and negatives. You should visit a franchise and stake it out, make a few purchases, and talk to the owners, management, employees, and customers.

Learn how much support franchises receive from the company. Franchisees can easily be found online or in Item 20 of the Franchise Disclosure Document (FDD). Since this can be such a life-changing decision, you may want to even consider getting a short-term job at a prospective franchise to get a feel of the business from the ground up. You might even work without pay.

Arrange to visit the franchisor's main headquarters and training center (Mister Donut called ours Donut U) to see how they run their day-to-day operation. Sometimes this is done in a group situation with other potential franchisees, called a discovery day, and is usually encouraged by reputable businesses. They want to find out who you are as much as you want to learn about them. Visiting numerous franchisor headquarters may rack up the frequent flyer miles, but it will be well worth it.

Printed franchise directories offering a summary of information can be a great place to begin. These include the Franchise

Opportunities Guide (published by the IFA), Franchise Update Publications, The Franchise Handbook, and Bonds Franchise Guide. The IFA website also has a "Find a Franchise" feature, allowing visitors to search by category, name, startup cash, investment, financing, availability, etc.

Great franchises feature irresistible, inexpensive products. For example:

- Hamburgers: Meat is expensive, but potatoes, shakes, and soda are cheap.
- Donuts: Ingredients are relatively cheap, as is coffee and soda.
- Chicken: Clucking fast food perfection. These stores didn't even open until 4:00 p.m. for take-out dinners and closed by 8:00 p.m. Chicken stays well in keepers until sold.
- Pizza: Sold anytime, a wide variety of types, easy to make, with lots of pie makers to hire, utilizing low-cost ingredients.

Trade Shows and Networking

An old-school but highly effective way of researching your opportunities is to attend Start Your Own Business trade shows to meet perspective franchisors. Nothing beats a little face-time to get the feel of the people who run a business. You can often get a company's FDD, containing a huge amount of pertinent business information. You cannot even legally be sold a franchise at one of these shows, since a cooling-off period is legally required from the time you receive the FDD.

The International Franchise Expo is sponsored by the IFA and is the biggest collection of franchisors seeking new franchisees. Their largest shows are in Washington, DC (spring),

Los Angeles (fall), and Miami (winter). These expositions are also great opportunities to learn about franchising in general from educational programs conducted by top industry professionals. Other trade shows include those organized by National Franchise & Business Opportunities.

Be careful at these shows, however. A startup that offers little track record can be a risky choice, even with the best of intentions. The same problems exist with fad products that may be here today and long gone tomorrow—along with your money.

Like with most other businesses, networking can be very important to successful franchising. Join professional organizations and other groups that are pertinent and can add something to your operations. I was always open to new ideas and therefore always learned from these groups. I was a joiner type, got along well, liked people as well as ideas, and sought out new concepts.

Teaching is another great way to share, so I volunteered for different kinds of work at conferences, fairs, and meetings in the United States, as well as in places such as Yugoslavia, Poland, Germany, England, and Asia. I served on committees at the US Department of Labor and the Commerce Department and also on many boards, such as the New England SBA, and was even considered for a major position in the SBA.

Compare this to the participation of an executive of an older, very successful company, Burger Chef, which went out of business after it sold out to a large NYSE food company. Frankly, I don't recall why, but I had invited him to speak on location acquisition, selection, etc. at the Boston College Franchise Center seminar. He agreed, but when it was his time to speak, he took the podium and laughed that he would never disclose such information and stepped down. Of course he was never asked to speak again, and I never saw him make any other public appearances. A panel was instantly formed without a second of delay to replace him, and the subject was thoroughly covered, but the executive was toast. Burger Chef itself also went out of business. I still don't know why he ever agreed to speak in the first place.

The moral of the story is you can't bury your head and expect to grow. The message from that is "I can't be bothered," and believe me, you won't be. The message gets across loud and clear: "Don't bother me, and I won't bother you." What could be worse for the future of your business? Although you won't be bothered, you also will not learn anything or benefit from anyone influential recommending you or your company for anything.

Asking the Right Questions

To find out what the reality of the business proposition you are being offered truly is, check in on at least a half-dozen existing franchisees to get opinions with a little realistic street credibility. Don't worry about the top operators running multiple stores; check in instead on the smaller and medium-size franchisees that are walking in shoes more or less similar to yours.

But keep in mind that these franchisees have already chosen and invested in the franchisors and are not anxious to knock them because it also knocks the franchisees themselves. They're partial toward the franchisor and their own investment, having already made the investment. But if you ask the right questions and keep asking when you sense a weak answer, the truth will be exposed. It's the best source. Your own demeanor should not be that of a prosecutor but a future cohort. You, too, want to invest and be a franchisee. You are very anxious to become part and want to be as proud as this franchisee is. That attitude should give you a clue as to his or her pleasure or displeasure.

Owners of multiple stores offer strong proof the franchise and its system is a good one—but keep asking questions. You'll get the answers even with the partiality if you keep asking, and even with the multi owners you'll uncover some weaknesses you can then discuss with the franchisor and perhaps avoid yourself.

- Would they invest again if they had the chance to do it all over?
- Where are the weaknesses?
- What qualities must a franchisee have besides money?
- Everything can't be perfect, so what should you look for and not repeat?
- How could the franchisor improve?
- What should you make sure you receive?
- How can you save some cash?
- Who are the strongest advisors that they respect the most, and who would you be better off avoiding if possible?
- Did they have to take the location offered, or could they have passed on it? If they passed, what would have happened? Would they get another opportunity right then, soon thereafter, or a year later, and would it be in proximity or two states away?
- Who are the best suppliers and why?
- What should they look out for with suppliers?

The rest of the questions should come naturally to you. Being smart enough to have saved the funds you are contemplating investing is adequate assurance. You'll ask plenty of the right questions and get good answers, so just don't give up. They were you once, and you just want to avoid obvious pitfalls. Believe me that there are no bad questions, no matter how dumb you think they might be. Every question leads to an answer, triggering another question. Explain that you just want to do as well as they have and be among the best.

To get the most out of these interviews and not waste anybody's valuable time, especially your own, make an appointment and prepare your questions in advance. Get the scoop concerning locations, costs, labor availability, and various common problems. How close to projected costs to get up and running was their business, and how soon until they (hopefully) reached a positive cash flow, including taking a reasonable salary for themselves? Perhaps the most important question to ask is: if they had it to do all over again, would they? If so, would they be interested in investing in your business and serving as your consultant? You may not want or need this, but the answer will be telling. Break down with him or her what the franchise opportunity really costs, not just how long to break even but how much you could possibly lose. Can you limit any personal liability of the financed portion? Can you limit any personal liability of the cash portion? Do they know anyone who closed or is struggling? You should talk to them as well.

Although most franchises have a proven record of success, there are many warning signs to watch out for. A high failure rate or quick turnover during the first few years of over 5 percent is a very ominous sign. Find out the reasons, but without an amazing explanation it is probably best to run for the hills. Other signs of trouble include if there are a lot of lawsuits pending, a bankruptcy history, or frequent corporate name changes. If the franchisor seems to be rushing to sign you up, does not properly check your financial qualifications, or is too new, you may also be in trouble.

The Red Flag Warnings

The waters are shark infested in the business world, so here are a few tips to avoid getting bitten.

- No rushing: Franchisors should not be trying to rush you into making a decision. The good ones want you to make a careful choice, as much for their own self-interests as your own.
- No FDD: Since federal law requires this, you should too. The franchisor should have no reluctance to provide the disclosure documents since there is significant financial liability for not supplying them. This is necessary to answer most of the questions below.
- Anemic financials: Have a qualified CPA help you study the three years of financials available in the FDD. Manage your level of risk by knowing theirs.
- Big turnover rate: If franchisees are often running away, perhaps you should be too. Item 20 of the FDD will answer how many franchises have jumped ship over the past three years.
- Be a legal eagle: Check out if your franchise is involved in too many lawsuits, found in Item 3 of the FDD. Another warning sign is if a franchisor is trying to avoid your bringing your own attorney to the table.
- Franchisee hell: If your predecessors are complaining, chances are you will be, too, at some point in the future.

What the Franchisor Should Provide

All franchisors are different, so be certain in advance what services they will provide if you go into business with them. They should let you know the financial requirements and provide market demographic information. Once you sign on the dotted line, they should provide their brand's trademarks and, if they are not providing the site, assist in selecting a site and offer construction and unit design help. They should also assist with supply sources, licenses, operations manuals and training programs, and grand openings.

To keep your franchise thriving, advertising and marketing plans, web pages, inventory control, financial reports, personal inspections on site, and operations updates are ongoing. At Mister Donut, our computers tracked the usage of all major products in every store, and by comparing periodic usages, we could tell franchisees if and where they were experiencing shortages, which could mean short delivery quantities or employee stealing.

When Mister Donut told franchisees to "do it our way or it could be the highway," it often created antagonism at first. The mistrust came from the franchisee assuming that the franchisor was making decisions based on their own profit, so some still tried shortcuts. But rather than save dollars, these shortcuts usually lowered quality and made for an inferior product. It took many positive results to get the point across that success was mutual. Squeezing the last buck out through shortcuts is not smart.

There was even an adversarial relationship when the IFA began, with a policy of no franchisee need apply. Today, however, franchisees are welcomed with open arms and considered true partners. Indeed, franchisees have been presidents of the IFA.

Hiring a Franchise Consultant or Broker

At least initially, you don't need a franchise consultant. A good certified public accountant (CPA), however, who is an expert in small business accounting is very valuable. Originally, franchisors didn't like franchisee consultants and advisors or any other intermediaries for that matter because, frankly, their focus is to find something wrong. A broker may also be more interested solely in his or her commission than in protecting you. A CPA knows as much or more and is likely to stay on with you for years.

Brokers are usually paid by franchisors to present prospects to them, so no fee is likely required from a potential franchisee. However, this arrangement could possibly tip the scales away from you for obvious reasons. Of course, there are many conscientious brokers, too, who are not paid by the franchisor they recommend, but the potential for conflict still exists.

Your research is obviously important, and you don't have many (if any) contract options anyway with most franchisors since it would be awkward having differing deals with franchise owners who frequently meet and may compare arrangements with each other.

Buying an Existing Franchise

Purchasing an established franchise may be a great way to jump-start your career. One might be found through the franchisor, an accountant or lawyer, or by placing an Internet, newspaper, or franchising magazine advertisement. Digging and having patience is the key to finding the right deal and could prove to be very positive.

Certain company-owned operations may be available from the franchisor as well. It is easier to evaluate the future from the history of a preexisting franchise than from one that never opened at all. You can build on their positive reputation.

The franchisor usually charges a transfer fee for its time, expenses, and training, but it is often worth it.

Assuming it's a profitable franchise, what is that profit worth?

Be sure to check the term of the transferred contract since it could be only a short remainder of the existing contract. If the seller has not already done so, check with the franchisor to see if a full-length contract is available and, if so, at what price. If you want to sell in the future, you will need to have an extension period to provide a buyer and assurance from the franchisor of another re-extension period.

You will still need approval from the home office to buy an existing franchise, but this can be a worthwhile shortcut to success. A proven track record makes financing easier and comes with an existing location, equipment, staff, and customer base. This is the equity I've talked about that a franchise allows you to build up. It's like jumping right in to the deep end of the pool, and you'll be in business and earning money immediately.

Be very careful, however, to understand why the sale is taking place in the first place. Is it underperforming or requiring improvements soon? Is there a bad lease or declining demand?

What Makes a Good Location?

Real estate is the backbone of much of the franchise business, and different locations work best for different types of businesses. Professionals such as lawyers, CPAs, investment advisors, and others charging for their services locate in major high rises or other commercial spaces.

Food chains require an expert opinion. Intuition alone is

inadequate. For instance, did you know that a far corner from a traffic light is a better location than the near corner (less congestion and more visibility offering time to stop and pull in and ease of ingress and egress.)? And don't forget the need for adequate and easy parking since some will avoid parking in congested lots. Drive-thru windows are now important, even though they didn't exist years ago.

Some of the issues that need to be addressed in a location include getting a detailed traffic count, specifying the number and type of vehicles, women in cars, children, traffic lights, congestion, visibility, ingress, and egress. This all comes after availability and costs for the location have been determined.

There are so many important variables, such as changes in areas such as highway traffic, business or residential changes, or new competition that hurts revenues. These and other commonsense questions can have a dramatic impact on the business's future survival.

Modern location scouting utilizes sophisticated geographic information systems software that includes consumer-trend and census data for every area of the nation. Demographic reports are easy to purchase online, providing much of the information needed to make intelligent decisions about geographic regions, including population, income, lifestyles, traffic flow, etc. You can even get the information on Google.

In an established franchise company, there always seems to be a little tension between the operations department that runs company stores and supervises franchise stores and the franchise and real estate departments. With everyone wanting to do well, if the unit sales are marginal, poorer, or even okay but still lower than planned, the real estate department tends to blame the ops people for poor management or supervision. The ops people blame the location and point out its faults, such as poor signage (even though the signage may have been the best the town would allow), and everybody blames the franchisee. The poor franchisee defends himself or herself as best he or she can, especially if no real estate is involved, but since he or she is the proverbial "low person on the totem pole," his or her opinion does not carry much weight.

This is the main reason farming out franchise sales can be a real problem. Why would anyone care if there was a bad apple in the bunch when they are paid only for placing the client? That's why my companies never paid commissions for such operations.

As Mister Donut grew, I used more and more regional real estate brokers. I would funnel local broker site inquiry presentations to brokers and kept them busy evaluating and making continuous commissions. That encouraged them to spend a lot of time digging for information, such as zoning, real estate investors, financing availability from banks, and other financial sources. The few favored regional brokers were involved in the majority of deals. In fact, one founder of one of the leading franchisors eventually married the company's most productive regional broker.

Selecting a location can be as difficult as it is crucial for success. There are many different types of locations available, including shopping malls, which vary greatly in and of themselves. Anchored by major chain stores, malls have parking that is usually plentiful, and traffic in the area is usually consistently strong; however, real estate prices at malls are at a premium, and management rules and restrictions apply. A neighborhood mall is usually anchored by a major supermarket and much more reasonable with rent and regulations. Community centers are larger and offer room for small freestanding buildings known as out-parcels. Lifestyle centers are found in more affluent areas, featuring high-end retailers as anchors, with higher rent for stores. Several big box stores (Wal-Mart, Home Depot, etc.) anchor power centers. Other types of shopping centers are found in various locations featuring numerous themes, including bargain outlet centers.

There are other alternate areas that can be considered as locations for certain types of franchises offering captive audiences, such as public transportation hubs, sports stadiums, colleges, hospital, hotels, etc. If these institutions are seasonal, however, your business will be as well.

Another trend for the last thirty years is dual branding, where different types of franchises are located next to each other or even in the same store, often all owned by the same parent company (for instance, Dunkin' Donuts and Baskin Robbins, or KFC, Pizza Hut, Taco Bell, and Long John Silvers). This can be a very efficient way to utilize kitchen, storage, and service space, especially if different products are in demand during specific times of the day.

One important final concept to understand about franchise location is the term "encroachment," where another similar store is opened too close to your business. Make certain you understand the terms of your contract and try to avoid this, both in terms of location and other non-bricks-and-mortar ways, such as sales by catalogue or on the Internet. Your territory is your livelihood, so make sure it is properly protected. The opposing reality is that there are "miracle miles" where many brands of car dealers or retail operations converge. There are bound to be similarities, even by the same chain, located on both sides of a divided main street, but the volume of business often warrants locating there.

Building a New Location

Creating a home for your new business may involve building from the ground up. This is a major area where the franchisor will offer a great deal of expertise and will have numerous design criteria that must be met without deviation. Each project requires selecting a top-notch architect and contractor and acquiring a myriad of permits, including variances, curb cut and signage authority, and certificates of occupancy. Then, of course, there is the price—as well as the final price. You can imagine the difference depending on the expertise of the developer. Franchise companies are expert developers, and they know how to get the most for the least. Mister Donut, and others, used regional contractors who were familiar with all the construction and permitting needs, which left no risk for the developer.

Mister Donut was the first company to develop prefabricated buildings to reduce the expense and speed up the construction period and opening of new stores. These two-thousand--square-foot fiberglass stores arrived at a new site in two huge parts, on flat bed trucks or trains then trucks, after the ground had been prepared and utilities were already stubbed up, ready for attachment, and our large road signs were ablaze.

Theses stores were in operation in less than a week, and, as a huge bonus, we were able to finance the building alone as a chattel, like a piece of equipment, significantly lowering the rent we had to pay for a land lease. We opened about twenty such stores, mostly in smaller locals. The prefabricated building was financed over seven years. The land leases were typically twenty years, with two additional ten-year options, so we saved thirteen years plus option times of the portion of rent that would have been required had the owner constructed the building. Once the shop was up and operational, the public couldn't tell it was prefabricated—and if they could, it didn't register with them as a negative.

5
Show Me the Money

When looking to crunch numbers, remember you are not in this alone. The franchisor shows you how much startup and ongoing expenses are, so there will be no guesswork or unpleasant surprises on your part. This is another important contribution a franchisor has to offer and, as pointed out, is an important reason to buy a franchise.

Starting a business is expensive. The corporate website of McDonald's states: "Generally, we require a minimum of $750,000 of non-borrowed personal resources to consider you for a franchise. Individuals with additional funds may be better prepared for additional or multi-restaurant opportunities." But there's a financial level for everybody out there seeking to enter the franchising world based on what one can afford.

An average franchise today goes for between $100,000 and $300,000, with 35 to 50 percent liquidity, or cash, but no matter how small your pocketbook, there is still probably a franchising opportunity out there for you. The polar opposite of the McDonald's Goliath would be an outfit like Jan-Pro Cleaning Systems, which requires only one thousand dollars in capital to join their commercial cleaning services empire. You can jump into fitness franchise Jazzercise with only $3,000.

Others seeking your business can help along the way.

The landlord usually provides some, if not all, leasehold improvements just to get your franchise for the benefit of his or her other space, and equipment can be financed through multiple sources and sometimes with the help of an equipment supplier. Typically, the franchisor will have these sources arranged.

Working capital is one area that is often significantly underestimated by newcomers. This is your fair warning: insufficient cash flow is a recipe for disaster. Don't take undercapitalization casually because figuring out just how much is enough is an important make-or-break judgment call. Working capital requirements are determined by understanding the amount of real cash needed to survive the initial opening costs and losses until operations become positive.

What good is having an excellent location, fully equipped, staffed, and ready to open, if from the start the anticipated revenues are less than planned and you run out of funds to survive? Consider that if the day you open, the stock market plunges 50 percent or some other financial tragedy pokes out its ugly head. As Murphy's Law states, if anything can go wrong, it probably will, and a financial cushion for emergencies is an absolute necessity for any new business. It is safest to assume you will be losing money for the first year.

How much capital is enough? Every situation is different, but six months of cash in the bank just to pay the basic bills that are pre-known, without you drawing a penny, is a minimum even if things go well. The unplanned out-of-pocket expenses that will definitely arise mount very rapidly.

While working every conceivable job in your fledgling business, including bathroom duty when the designated staff member doesn't show up and there's no one else to appoint, may not be the glamorous mogul life you envisioned, it's important to stay realistic. I've seen people make all kinds of crazy projections, such as having their new Cadillac delivered on opening day. A week later, the celebratory vacation begins. Then the manager quits after the first week, the revenues are low, and the whole investment that was foolishly predicated on immediate positive cash flow turns out to be just the opposite. Uh-oh. Meanwhile, the new owner vacations a thousand miles away, oblivious to his crumbling new empire. In no time the operation closes, and the franchisor must decide whether to take it over or let it close.

No franchisor would knowingly permit something like this, but they don't require your bank statements, just proof of adequate capital. They tell you of your financial needs and personal commitment, but you have to take it from there. Don't open a new business if you don't have the reserves and working capital to survive a poor (or worst-case scenario) first year.

Once you begin to narrow down your options, it's time to study the franchise agreement and all other legal documents. For example, Item 7 of the FDD presents typical startup expenses, including the initial franchise fee, construction, décor, equipment and fixtures, landscaping, insurance, and inventory. Figure out what it takes to run the franchise for at least six months and budget from there to play it safe.

Franchisor Income

Keep in mind that the continuing income from franchisees to franchisors derives from the periodic payment of a percentage of the operations sales called royalties, which grow slowly until the franchise chain grows. The initial franchise fee is developed to cover the cost of selling the franchise, which includes media, advertising, public relations, franchise exhibitions, arranging for the location, selecting the equipment, training of the franchisee, and opening the store. Thus royalties for the franchisor are low until there are perhaps twenty-five to fifty operations, limiting the speed of growth to just a few stores per year in the initial few years.

Companies that rapidly expand are subject to high costs and less-experienced staff who are slower to identify problems and solve them quickly. The same goes for financing. You may have access to deep funds, but until you have excess funds from operating income, which has no interest cost, you may require every dollar you can secure. If something can go wrong, it probably will. During the savings and loan debacle of the 1980s and 1990s, bank financing for franchises practically disappeared. Additionally, the recent recession reinforced this liquidity problem.

Cost Breakdown

The initial franchise fee is paid before opening, one time, if not financed by the franchisor. The amount of this fee can be found on most franchisors' websites or through contacting their home offices. The fee can range from a few hundred dollars to $1 million, with an average of about $25,000. A higher or lower fee may not reflect the quality of a franchise, although most of the bigger brands demand more capital. This fee usually includes the price of corporate training.

All other costs are, of course, yours, which include rent, taxes, utilities, remodeling, equipment, supplies and inventory, labor, uniforms, license, and permit fees. Your franchisor will have them all itemized.

Royalties are usually a continuous monthly periodic fee paid to the franchisor, typically 5 percent to 12 percent of the gross revenues, and are nonnegotiable. Advertising and marketing fees are typically around 2 percent of gross revenues. You generally pay for grand opening marketing and other associated costs. Giveaway items of products or merchandise can often total twenty-five thousand dollars or more. Advertising fees are used to support all of the franchises in the system and can sometimes operate on a sliding scale. Also occasionally there is a monthly minimum fee.

Add to that working capital of up to a year, and you can see the costs totaling up higher than you might have originally expected. One of the advantages in the franchise world is utilizing the buying power of the system to reduce some of these costs. Some equipment items may be purchasable pre-owned at a reduced cost.

In today's world, there are ever-growing work-at-home opportunities in franchising. These not only offer convenience but are also significantly less costly. Some of the major expenses, such as real estate and remodeling, are completely eliminated.

Case Study: Mister Donut's Marketing, Advertising, and Promotion

The typical franchise prospect considers advertising and promotion a cost, but it really should be looked at more like a benefit. It is beyond a bargain, assuming it's fairly accounted for. For example, think of the Dunkin' Donuts advertising campaign that each franchise pays 2 percent of sales toward. "Time to make the donuts" is a catchy slogan that is still remembered today—likewise for McDonald's "You deserve a break today," Burger King's "Have it your way," "Avis, we try harder," and Mister Donut's "We put our heart in it."

Advertising and brand-name recognition are great benefits you derive from a franchise. Sometimes new franchisors require little, if any, advertising contribution until there are an adequate number of franchises that can generate a meaningful fund. The brand is built significantly through advertising and local recognition.

Promotion is an essential aspect of driving your market share as well. Public relations is considered by many to be more important than advertising, which it surely is in the early years of a business when there is only a small advertising budget. One of the best examples of this was when Mister Donut did a giveaway of free franchises on the number-one primetime television game show, *The Price Is Right*. The cost to us was zero because Goodson-Todman Productions, the producers of the show, wanted to do such a unique giveaway. But who would have known this fact until we tried what many considered a complete waste of time? This was a big turning point for the company and put us in the big leagues of the franchise business. That Mister Donut was the first such franchise on primetime television, on Sunday night at 8:00 p.m., resulting in franchise inquiries and location offers, as well as considerable media attention. It was nothing short of amazing.

For four weeks, at a marginal cost, Mister Donut gave away a "Business of Your Own," a free franchise with a twenty-year turnkey lease of a fully equipped ready-to-open shop under a normal franchise agreement with the usual royalties and fees. The initial franchise fee and equipment costs were reimbursed through a higher lease/rent charge. If the company had to pay for the actual airtime, we could not have possibly afforded it.

In a subsequent marketing coup, Mister Donut capitalized on our slogan, "We put our hearts in it" by making heart-shaped holes and heart-shaped donuts and giving out "We put our hearts in it" lapel pins at every store. At that time, AVIS was running a promotion: "We Try Harder." We made a reciprocal deal with AVIS to give away a year's use of AVIS car rentals during a four-week drawing. We advertised with eight-foot posters with a photo of the car in the window of every Mister Donut shop, and in turn AVIS gave away "We put our heart in it" Mister Donut pins at every counter worldwide.

Another example of simple, inexpensive promotion was at a business conference in Las Vegas, where I provided twenty-five dozen fresh donuts for all attending, obtained from the Mister Donut shop there. One attendee recalled that it motivated him to buy a few years later and open some forty franchises throughout the State of Virginia for my then-latest franchise endeavor, Sizzleboard.

We also published a freestanding magazine insert in Sunday *Boston Globe* newspapers for our hundredth Mister Donut store opening. It included pictures of our management team as well as a company history. This was very unique then, and we parlayed it to propel even bigger growth, using the insert thereafter as our brochure for franchising. The 1960s was over fifty years ago, and back then one hundred store chains was a rare event and garnered a great deal of acknowledgement. Unique magazine inserts into Sunday papers were also new and infrequent, then typically the sole insert in the newspaper, as compared with today, when multiple inserts fill the inside of the Sunday paper.

Advertising and promotion combine to be the hot button of franchising, reaching multiple potential audiences: franchisee prospects, investors, real estate brokers and developers (including mall and shopping center developers), banks and financing agencies, and suppliers and retail customers.

As part of Mister Donut's efforts to expand internationally, we were able to promote both our company and our country simultaneously. We made arrangements with the US Department of Commerce (at their cost) to exhibit in world trade shows in London, England; Frankfort, Germany; Zagreb, Yugoslavia;

and Poznan, Poland. We included a large backdrop of photos of every franchise owner and their locations in the United States, demonstrating that in America anyone can own their own business. The publicity was significant, including a *Boston Globe* feature article written by me, reprinted and distributed to potential franchise prospects with the Sunday insert.

These are just a few of the opportunities we created to showcase, exemplify, spotlight, and identify Mister Donut. These endeavors were well received and turned out to be important to growth. They also served to distinguish us.

As Mister Donut grew rapidly, I was always seeking creative ideas to support and improve our image. Today it looks natural, easy, and intuitive, but back then during our humble beginnings such ideas were new and innovative. The exact worth of each promotion is hard to evaluate but essentially priceless.

Today, a great deal of franchise advertising is developed at the dealer's direction, by a committee of dealers, with the advertising cost collected by the franchisor. The multiple audiences likely included possible corporate buyers. For example, Mister Donut became one of the first franchisors to be acquired by the New York Stock Exchange giant.

The Bottom Line

The big question you are probably asking yourself by now is, "How much will I be earning?"

What is traditionally called an "earnings claim" may appear in the FDD, but only a small percentage of franchisors actually report it, and most will not make such claims in writing if a franchisee doesn't reach levels specified. They avoid profit claims so that they will not be liable for a lawsuit later on. There are too many business variables for them, and not all franchisees are created equally. If a franchise makes an earnings claim, make sure you understand its basis and if it was prepared by an outside CPA. Study the fine print disclaimers to know what these numbers actually mean.

You can calculate revenues yourself by checking the franchise's audited financial statement in the FDD under "Franchise Royalties." Divide this number by the amount of non-company-owned outlets to determine the average-per-franchise revenue. Divide that by the franchise's royalty rate and viola! You have now determined the average gross per store.

Financing Options

The best financial term to seek out is probably the longest term, with the cheapest interest rate and lowest down payment, though some prefer no debt and have enough financial strength to go without. I only saw this once, but nevertheless it exists. Financing is always about the same for franchises, so rates are very competitive. Call the current bank you do business with, or any bank for that matter, and tell them you're going into business and require financing. The fact is that you need to shop around. The more cash you put in, the lower the rate and better the terms.

The Small Business Administration (SBA) also helps put people in business and has assisted in the financing of a large number of franchisees. Although they do not actually lend money, they do provide a guarantee of 90 percent of a bank loan and usually longer payout terms and thus lower monthly payments, so that's the best place to begin. An SBA-approved franchise is more easily accepted for a loan. Their Franchise Registry program features tools to improve and increase loans to franchisees. Franchisors are provided access to various lenders, and lenders are provided with the information they need to underwrite SBA and conventional loans.

Licensed and regulated by the SBA, Small Business Investment Companies (SBICs) are another possible opportunity for financing. These are private companies, and each makes its own rules of how it provides equity capital. Some provide money only, others equity plus loans in return for a piece of your business.

Pre-qualifying with a lender prior to deep involvement with a franchisor will help you further understand just how much financial burden you can afford to take on. This enables you to jump on the right opportunity when it comes along. Keep in mind that you require enough liquidity for a 20-percent to 30-percent down payment of the total initial investment in order for a lender to even take a first look at your paperwork.

There are two ways to finance a business: debt and equity. Debt financing means you borrow the money in a loan that must be paid back with interest. Equity financing comes from an investor, who then owns a percentage of your business. There is no need to repay this person except from the sale of a business, but you must split a percentage of the profits that are paid out to investors based on the percent of the equity you agreed to share with them. This can sometimes lead to conflicts if the partners are not properly matched. Franchisees rarely have equity partners, except perhaps family members who help by advancing capital. Large financings, like hotel franchises, are more likely to involve equity partners.

Banks or other similar lending institutions are the most common approach to such financing. The familiarity of a major franchise often makes getting a loan much easier since they know the system has a successful track record. If there is a previous relationship with the franchisor or other franchisees, that may speed up the project. Franchises affiliated with the Franchise Registry make it substantially easier to get an SBA loan. All lenders will need to see what collateral you have to guarantee their loan, and you'll usually be asked to sign a personal guarantee.

So first take a serious look at your own finances to see what you can afford and don't forget to bring your family in on this discussion. Your spouse's financial comfort level can make the difference during a stressful launching period. Accurately assessing your financial situation and tolerances is the most important step in determining your budget for starting a new business. Since life and business are both unpredictable, you must make sure you leave yourself a sizeable nest egg to fall back on.

Another group of equity investors are "angel" investors who exchange startup funds for a piece of the business. There are often strings attached in the form of more active involvement. This could actually be a good thing for a business newbie. This type of partnership can take some of the power out of your hands, requiring their approval for certain day-to-day decisions, however, so be particularly careful with whom you choose to allow to be your angel.

A growing means of modern financing is coming from the franchisors themselves. Check to see if your company offers such programs since they have long-established relationships with lending institutions or offer loans directly. Over 20 percent of all franchisors are now offering such a program, often the newer and smaller ones. Franchisors are developing creative techniques that are worthy of exploring, such as co-investing with you or deferring payments.

There are also some government grants available for small business that can be found at the SBA's website. Low-interest programs are also available in some states.

Minorities and Women

Some franchisors offer minority owners special financial programs, such as the Southland Corporation (7-Eleven) and Burger King. Working closely with minority organizations such as the National Association for the Advancement of Colored People (NAACP) has helped many franchisors with recruitment. The IFA Educational Foundation's Diversity Institute was formed in 2006 "to increase the number and success of minorities in franchising, including franchisors, franchisees, suppliers, and employees."

According to the SBA, women wholly own approximately 10 percent of US franchises and about 30 percent as part of a family ownership. It is a mystery why the numbers have remained so small despite the opportunity being so big and the fact that certain types of franchises offer more family time to their owners than other sorts of businesses. Some types of businesses have proven more attractive to females, such as gyms and day care, but overall they do not seem to show the desire to own a business as strongly as men have in the past.

The Women's Franchising Committee (WFC) of the IFA was formed in 1996 and "is dedicated to inspiring and encouraging women in franchising by creating a network of business professionals dedicated to strengthening the success of women in franchising." The WFC offers programs and resources to achieve this, including everything from how-to guides and conferences to local networking chapters.

6

Creating a Business Plan

Creating a business plan is essential when seeking money from others. This roadmap is designed to help ease the minds and open the wallets of everyone from friends and family to banks and investors. It also serves to help clarify ideas in your own head by creating clear goals. At best, however, it is a work in progress for any business. As life takes its usual twists and turns, business plans must evolve and change with the times.

Your franchisor may be able to help you design a business plan, and there are numerous books and websites to learn the proper form. Your CPA might also have the adequate document. Obtaining a copy of a previously successful plan from another franchisee would be an ideal inspiration to learn from. Those who have gone before you would also be very helpful in projecting income and cash flow for your operation. Some franchisors may also be able to supply you with such a sample plan.

The most important part of your plan is the projection of financials, including the income statement, cash-flow statement, and balance sheet. Operating results from one area, however, may be quite different in another.

Planning Time

There's obviously a lot to do before you open your doors on the first day of your new business, so there's no reason to rush in amateurishly. Take your time to thoroughly research your options, draw up appropriate plans, and then make your selection. It can take a year or two from the moment you make a business selection until your grand opening. More complicated business ventures can require twice as much time or even more.

Recognize the value of market research. Conduct an analysis of the industry you are seeking to enter, as well as an examination of the individual local market. Franchisors can be a big help in understanding both. From the data you gather, you can come to more intelligent, educated conclusions of your own.

Consider the physical toll of starting up such a new business as well. Are you up for twelve-hour days, seven days a week, if that's what it takes to get the party started? Self-motivation, positivity, and intense endurance and energy are job requirements, especially during the most difficult periods.

So be wise in your research and be patient in your process in order to achieve franchise success.

Case Study: Omnidentix

Around 1980, I started a new franchised chain in the walk-in, retail dental center business called Omnidentix, proving that opening a dentist franchise was not unlike a donut shop. It was the first of its kind in the world, although Sears had a few dental centers in a few West Coast stores. Those were offered to us, but we declined because the locations on the second floor near the return section were poor, relative to what we thought our needs were for adequate revenues. Omnidentix required center court locations for maximum exposure. We began by opening eight two-thousand-square-foot operatory centers in high and dense retail locations in Boston and soon had about fifteen duplicate centers on the East Coast to South Florida and west to Chicago.

Using the Omnidentix system franchise as an example to understand the typical franchise fee process, the initial fee in 1980 was fifty thousand dollars, of which twenty-five thousand dollars was paid in cash and the balance financed over five years, likely out of the income from the individual dental practice. In addition, a continuing royalty comprising of combined real estate and management fees totaled thirty-five thousand dollars annually and was charged regardless of gross sales.

In general, franchises that generated $600,000 in annual sales would pay a fee of approximately 6 percent. If the franchise generated $1 million annually, the fee would be 3 percent. The main reason Omnidentix adopted the same charge for every franchise was to treat all of them equally and in recognition that larger volume units usually do not receive or require additional services. As a matter of fact, a better argument could be made that lower volume sales usually require the most home office attention.

Assuming a fifteen-year renewable franchise agreement, the total charges would amount to an initial fee of $50,000 and an annual fee of $35,000, payable in twelve equal monthly installments for fifteen years, totaling $525,000. The current cash value discounted at 6 percent per annum would be approximately $200,000 for a total of $250,000 before income taxes.

A local century-old bank in Boston, which had financed some dentists who opened Omnidentix in the city, offered us a $5-million loan to open company-operated dental centers, payable with interest only for five years on outstanding terms. We bit, but with nearly $4 million of the $5 million spent or committed on construction of a ring of eight dental centers surrounding Chicago, the bank (which had changed from a savings bank to an S&L during this period) failed. We were not in default and had over $1 million in cash remaining from a recent public offering but nevertheless could not deal with or meet the government bureaucrats' demands. Omnidentix had to stop franchising while the bank and hundreds of other S&L banks failed across the United States.

Some of those Omnidentix offices became the start of other dental chains, while others just changed their names and got out from under their financing. Today, there are dental centers in nearly every mall and high-traffic retail street in America. Check your Yellow Pages to see how many large ads there are for dental chains. When we opened our first few centers, state dental boards threatened the company with whatever they could dream up. In an effort to scare away dentists from the company, they tried to cancel the dental licenses of dentists practicing in an Omnidentix. This occurred even with the attorney general advising them in writing that the US Supreme Court decided the case preventing their actions.

When we were launching this operation, I was asked to be on NBC's *Today* show with Bryant Gumble. A dentist who also served on the Massachusetts Dental Board was brought on to debate me. He denigrated the dental centers and the dentists who worked in them. When Gumble asked me to respond to the secretary's comments, I reported how surprised I was that he would say anything negative about Omnidentix because he had actually discussed with me buying an Omnidentix franchise. Actually, he probably would have been a very good franchise owner.

Gumble was shocked and asked the secretary for confirmation. He acknowledged he had spoken with me, and we discussed a franchise for him, and he immediately added that he didn't mean to include Omnidentix in his description. He declared that we were the exception. Of course, that was the end of the interview, and the Massachusetts State Dental Board dropped their proceedings against the dentists.

The Legal Issues

Make sure you have thoroughly read and understood all legal agreements and information prior to signing. This can best be accomplished by selecting an experienced franchise attorney. Find one through recommendations, and the best place to start is by calling the International Franchise Association and the American Bar Association's Forum on Franchising to begin setting up interviews. The Bar Association also provides many valuable sources and articles. Franchise Update publishes "The Directory of Franchise Attorneys," and you can also reach out to other franchisees to follow up anecdotally. Although the primary document is required to be written in "plain English," it is still essential to have an attorney's experienced and educated eyes review the contract and advise you concerning what you are signing up to do and not do and to find what the costs and liabilities are.

Case Study: Mister Donut, Esquire

Franchising, as it is known today, was essentially new when I started. Its freshness and the opportunities it presented to start a business were the forces that drove me to it. With such an innovative and motivating idea, along with my law degree, I felt I would make up for the disadvantage I felt in being so young and inexperienced.

Franchising as a business started out in its original form

with what I referred to earlier as "management by accident." No one knew what they were doing and just went from situation to situation, good and bad. So if one of the first franchise prospects wanted to franchise a whole state with ten dollars down, decisions had to be made since there was no standard. Or if the territorial protection demanded against adding a second or more Mister Donut franchises in a nearby radius protection, a decision also had to be made.

We eventually standardized the area protection as a two-mile radius of the site. Eventually it was reduced to two miles in either direction on the same side of the same major street on which the shop was being opened. It was recognized that parallel arteries were a different territory for fast food shopping (for example, a cup of coffee and two donuts), and if we didn't locate there our competition eventually would.

Even some ten years later, franchising still seemed new. When we opened in Japan, for example, everything in the store had to be much smaller because space was dramatically more expensive. For example, we had two thirty-six-inch fryers in each kitchen in America, and we had tried to reduce their size to save money on equipment and make donut cooking take longer so they would always be fresher. We could not accomplish this in the United States because primarily, among other objections, bakers wouldn't support such a reduction. Such a decrease in capacity would have made for longer baking hours, and we were equally as interested in clean stores and trained sales staff. Obviously we could have insisted but decided it was not worth the bad will that might exist. However, we had no choice in Japan—either we reduced sizes or we couldn't open.

In Japan, each shop has one twenty-four-inch fryer. Space was saved, equipment cost reduced, and donuts were fresher since they were made over a longer period of time and less vegetable oil was needed. Less cleaning was also a result, and the same shrinking happed in the entire shop, including reduced counter size. The result: higher sales.

There were many such "happy accidents" across the board since we had no roadmap and everything was by ear. Decisions were made as best they could be—and quickly—in every aspect of the business.

Another example of this was found in real estate with the leasing of locations, perhaps the most difficult and critical part of the business. The rules kept changing on the spot. Where I thought I could make a better or smarter deal, I made that decision on the fly, and thereafter that new detail became the norm. From paying a one-year rent security deposit returned at the end of the lease, security went to six months, then down to three, and eventually zero. Instead of paying rent against a percentage of sales, we evolved to only pay a portion based on higher sales and finally refused altogether, just like McDonald's. Still, sometimes we backed down.

The Franchise Disclosure Document

The Franchise Disclosure Document (FDD), formerly called the Uniform Franchise Offering Circular (UFOC), is a disclosure or offering statement that is the key legal document you will need to understand. Here's where the franchisor must disclose most of the pertinent information in writing concerning how their company operates and what exactly they are offering. This includes the franchise agreement, as well as any other pertinent financial statements and documents. The FDD came into existence several years after.

The FDD was developed to prevent the unscrupulous business practices of some early franchisors. Franchising fever was burning white hot in the mid-to-late 1960s, and some began taking advantage entering franchising. Watching those owning McDonald's and KFCs and the like become rich, potential franchisees began a virtual gold rush. Some companies sold franchises as quickly as possible even though they were growing at speeds that they could not possibly keep up with, and eventually quality began to suffer as a result. Various tactics were used to manipulate money out of people's pockets, such as hanging celebrity names over worthless businesses or even selling nonexistent franchises.

Some states stepped up with their own financial disclosure laws, with California leading the way. Finally, in 1979, the Federal Trade Commission (FTC) took charge and implemented national franchise disclosure standards. This marked the birth of a document that has grown and matured over the years, raising the industry's standards along the way and nurturing its growth. Franchises cannot even legally be sold until ten days after an FDD is presented. These documents must also be registered in fourteen states, and many other states require the filing of a notice.

Relationship laws also protect franchisees from unscrupulous franchisors, and nineteen states have laws to prevent unjust termination. Most also include renewal protection clauses, and the North American Securities Administrators Association (NASAA) sets guidelines concerning detailed information to be provided.

Some of the key items you'll find in the current FDD include the franchisor's important staff members and their relevant backgrounds, bankruptcy and lawsuit history, and the fees required for owning and operating the franchise. The required initial investment and purchases, territorial rights, legal responsibilities, and financial statements are also included. In addition, the track record of previous franchises can be found and contact information for the successes and transfers. Much can also be learned from the failures and closings, the unhappy endings of former franchisees.

Once the FDD is completely studied and digested, there is a ten-business-day waiting period from the moment of the first face-to-face meeting with the franchisor, when the FDD is handed over, to the time when the franchisee can finally sign up. Once all of the blank spaces are filled in concerning your specific deal, you are still required to wait for a five-day cooling-off period.

The cover page of the FDD contains some common-sense basics, such as reminding you to read it thoroughly, seek the advice of a lawyer and accountant, and study your state's laws. This introduction also notes that the FTC has not examined the document, so they can't vouch for its accuracy. Check the date the document was created or updated and make certain it's recent.

Page two summarizes the offering plan and initial investment. Risks are also reviewed, such as choice of home-state law to govern over the contract, where franchisee may sue franchisor, and whether arbitration is available to settle disagreements. The audited financial statement is provided by the franchisor here as well.

There are twenty-three items contained within the rest of the document:

Item 1: The franchisor, their parents, predecessors, and affiliates
The company's basic information is provided, including how long they've been in business, address, and state of incorporation. Affiliates and predecessors are identified, as well as if they have ever used a different name to offer franchises (be careful if they have a history of name changes). Also any governmental regulation of the related industry is detailed.

Item 2: Business experience of key persons
The background of the directors, officers, and executives of the past five years is discussed.

Item 3: Litigation history
Pending or past relevant criminal and civil litigations against company executives are revealed, as well as if they have sued their franchisees.

Item 4: Bankruptcy
It's important to know if the company or its officers have declared bankruptcy in the last decade since that can dramatically affect their ability to take out loans to grow the business.

Item 5: Initial franchise fee
Before you open your doors to the public, this is the fee you will have to pay. It includes the cost of initial inventory, signs, equipment, leases, or rentals. Ongoing fees, such as royalties and advertising, are also reviewed. If all franchisees are not paying the same fee, this item explains how that is established.

Item 6: Other fees and expenses
Some of the additional monetary requirements are listed, including royalties, advertising contributions, training, transfer fees, audits, attorney charges, renewals, and anything else that the company will bill for.

Item 7: Initial investment
This chart includes the necessary startup costs, how those payments are to be made, and when they will be due. Some of the listed items include the franchise fee, training, lease, and improvements.

Item 8: Restriction on sources of products and services
This item explains what items must be purchased from the franchisor or its affiliates. This can be done to ensure quality control and can encompass a wide variety of items.

Item 9: Franchisee's obligations
This item is a list of some of the responsibilities of the franchisee. Although the details of each item are not discussed in this section, this will inform one where to find them. They can include a diverse list, such as site selection and development, lease or acquisition, training, fees, standards and policies, territorial development, maintenance, insurance, advertising, transfers, renewals, and various other obligations.

Item 10: Financing
If the company provides financial assistance, it can be found here. Terms and arrangements are spelled out, and sample financial agreements are often provided as part of the accompanying package.

Item 11: Franchisor's obligations
This section defines what the individual franchisor must supply. Training, advertising, and marketing plans before opening and follow-up throughout the course of the operation are essential to the success of a franchise and should be studied very carefully. Other important items include location scouting, computers and software, and electronic cash register use.

Item 12: Territory
How large is the contracted territory, and is it exclusive? If another branch of the same franchise is opened too nearby, it can dilute the value of the territory. Also addressed is how territories can be modified and expanded and if the territory can be shared or terminated due to poor performance.

Item 13: Trademarks
This discloses which trademarks are owned by the franchisor and any limits that come with them. This is the face of the system that is being purchased and creates the value of the brand.

Item 14: Patents, copyrights, and proprietary information
A successful franchisor's product is unique, and their intellectual property is in high demand, resulting in sales for the franchisee. This section demonstrates that they own all of the above.

Item 15: Participation in the actual operation of the franchise business
This section determines how involved the franchisee is actually required to be. Some require the franchisee to be completely hands-on, while others allow an absentee owner to leave the day-to-day business to an onsite manager.

Item 16: Restrictions on what the franchisee may sell
Limits and conditions on what can or can't be sold to customers are discussed in this item.

Item 17: Renewal, termination, transfers, and dispute resolution
This table defines the initial length of the contract, renewal, termination and transfer terms, and dispute resolution conditions (usually in the franchisor's state).

Item 18: Public figures
If celebrities or other public persons are involved in the promotion of the franchise, their payment, involvement, and investment are described here.

Item 19: Earnings claims
Since this section is not required, most franchisors do not provide it. Even if there is a claim to potential earnings based on similar franchises, it is not usually very helpful and should be verified by an independent CPA. If they don't disclose the numbers here, they can't legally disclose them anywhere else. Verbal bragging and boasting isn't worth the paper it's not printed on.

Item 20: Other franchise outlets
These charts provide information on other franchisees, including the total number of units and outlets that have closed or been transferred or sold the following year, as well as company-owned stores. Contact information for current franchises is listed, an important factor for follow-up research.

Item 21: Financial statements
The devil is in the details, as they always say, and you can find them in this section. With a qualified CPA's assistance, crunch these numbers to review the franchisor's audited financial statements and overall stability over the last several years. Analyze past and future growth potential, as well as the company's financial support for franchises and overall monetary resources.

Item 22: Contracts
All of the agreements you will need to sign are listed and should be attached. These include the franchise agreement, leases, options, purchase agreements, and financial documents.

Item 23: Receipt acknowledgement
Signing this page acknowledges that you have received the document, satisfying FTC requirements.

The Franchise Agreement

The Franchise Agreement is not to be confused with the information-packed FDD. The Franchise Agreement is a legally binding contract between the franchisee and the franchisor and does not contain the detailed information of the FDD. This separate document often accompanies the FDD and covers the initial and continuing fees, training renewal and termination terms, purchasing regulations, territory, advertising and marketing rules, and a great deal more. A trained and experienced franchise attorney best deciphers this document. You can't sign this document right away; you must legally wait five days from receipt.

There is usually very little wiggle room for negotiation of such contracts, and the agreements are very one-sided. Major changes are prohibited by what's presented in the FDD and would require refilling with the FTC. Any changes made for one franchise would then have to be offered for others, further complicating the issue.

Furthermore, a popular, well-established franchise simply has no reason to negotiate because of the demand for their business. It is to the average franchisee's benefit that the franchisor serves as the uniform enforcer so that other individual outlets will not reflect poorly on each other or the brand. Royalty rates are usually locked in stone, but there are some aspects an experienced franchise attorney may find a little give.

If there is a little room to negotiate, try to make sure your territory is well protected and you have the *right to cure* your own breaches of contract. A fair period to make such corrections is usually about thirty days so that you will not be easily tossed aside for minor violations. Other possible negotiations may include the schedule for franchise fee payment and extra training and support. Your renewal terms, as well as details on selling your franchise in the future, are occasionally open for discussion.

Though most franchise agreements are twenty years plus options, a fee may be inserted every five or ten years for many different reasons. Don't let these options force you to cancel. It's not worth the lawsuit time and expense and sends the wrong message of "you versus us."

The franchisee-franchisor relationship is a give-and-take proposition, and the reliable franchisor takes great pains to make sure that all the terms of the relationship, written and unwritten, are understood. It is important that the franchise agreement, like the marriage vow, must work mutually through thick and thin, through sickness and health.

Case Study: Mister Donut's Legal Saga

The most important chapter in the Mister Donut story is also a valuable lesson in dealing with the legal issues of franchising.

Howard Johnson's started as a local Boston hotdog stand and grew from there to a large, four-hundred-unit company, with 150-plus-seat restaurant chains as well as hundreds of motels/hotels throughout the United States. They even sold many products in supermarkets, such as hot dogs and ice cream.

In 1965, the company sold for nearly $400 million. The year I founded the Boston College Franchise Center, we gave our first Hall of Fame award to HoJo's and the second one to a newer comer called McDonald's.

Right from the beginning of our franchising, I was uncomfortable with the substance (not the language or structure) of one provision in the agreement we used. It was based on the one HoJo's had utilized and developed. The huge regard in which we held their company, and the fact it was a local restaurant chain, seemed to justify its use, especially since there weren't many others to serve as guides at that point in history.

The problem provision essentially provided that all products—food, paper, or otherwise—be purchased from/through their company. This was a great way to garner profits because the amount of the markups was small and secret, and the franchisee could benefit from the volume discounts the franchisor enjoyed.

This was also about the same time the IFA was formed, and as head of the IFA legal committee, I was responsible for pointing out legal issues. I took my responsibility seriously, and with the advice of my law school professors and other experts, I interviewed the best-regarded anti-trust lawyers in the country to represent the IFA, finally selecting Gerald Van Cise of Cahill Gordon & Reindel of New York City. He introduced me to Mary Gardner Jones, the head of the Federal Trade Commission, who became the keynote speaker at the First Boston College Franchise Center conference, and Gerald Van Cise was the moderator.

The main question they asked was, "Are your controls of your franchisees necessary?" I spoke at the first Start Your Own Business Show at the New York Coliseum, suggesting that franchisors should discuss the subject with their law firms with the goal of loosening restrictions, putting a better, overall fairer light on their franchise agreements.

Restrictions might prove acceptable during the initial startup period of the business until a foothold is established. However, a point is soon reached where requirements to purchase from the corporation may become illegal unless there really was a secret formula, like at Coca-Cola, which need not be disclosed.

Mister Donut's franchise agreement was pretty standard for the time, requiring every product to be purchased from or through our sources, with no exceptions—not just secret flour and even jellies, but basics like milk, cream, yeast, vegetable oil, salt, pepper, sugar, and even paper, boxes, bags, uniforms, and soap. It was a significant profit center for the company but reasonably could not be justified and was contrary to the Sherman, Clayton, and FTC Acts.

As I began to realize the growing problem, we were getting in deeper trouble each day as new shops rapidly opened. I feared it would all come crashing down as we reached nearly one hundred stores. If we showed weakness to just one franchisee, we could lose many or even lose the entire business.

We were competing neck and neck with Dunkin' Donuts, so I spoke to my counterpart there, Bob Rosenberg. Although I had been his camp counselor years earlier and liked him very much, it was not easy to match the great job he was doing with the quality team he built. My wife's father and Bob's father married sisters; we were a few years apart in age and essentially rarely were in contact. To me this legal problem was like life and death, but Bob thought I was overreacting to the legal aspects because I had a JD background and not an MBA like he had. Some years after, they changed their franchise agreement to one similar to ours. Mister Donut, ahead of the times, had been sold to International Multifoods (NYSE), the world's largest flour millers. I moved on, started a new franchise, Sizzleboard, and went public before the first restaurant even opened.

I had decided to face the legal issue early by changing our franchise agreements and hope for the best. I could see being put out of business over the issue, or at least paying out a fortune in settlements—in my minimum guess, everything we could earn over the next few years or so. But to live and grow with the problem was worse to me. I was only in my early thirties then.

First I made computer printouts of the exact purchases and income we derived from each franchisee to show each franchisee how much we made from their purchases and how much they might save buying on their own, using our volume-purchasing savings. This actually amounted to the equivalent of approximately 2 percent of their revenues. I proposed we would trade off requiring their purchasing exclusively from us in exchange for increasing their royalty payments by the same 2 percent. Nearly all were convinced they could save even more, and we knew in fact that they were already actually purchasing products other than those we sold them but never wanted to challenge them on. In other words, they were cheating on purchasing exclusively from us and figured they would come out a bigger winner than we thought with the new deal. In addition, I suggested we'd both save the time and fortune of many multi-year-long lawsuits over whether we could indeed operate as we did. It wasn't so cut and dry, except I had less confidence in our side of the argument, but they had to know we'd fight them if they violated their franchise agreement.

We had been tracking them and knew the facts. Though we never told them, we could have told them how much of every product they had to have purchased based on the revenue they reported, such as how much flour required a certain quantity of jellies, shortening, and sugar. The times we used these ratios was to tell our operations local supervisors when we thought there was a lot of stealing going on from certain franchisees, so they could help the franchises they supervised.

I began with the toughest and best franchisee, who had three successful shops. My thinking was that I knew him well, and everyone in the chain knew him from our periodic franchisee conferences and area meetings. If he signed the new agreement, he would broadcast the benefits to all, and many if not most of the others were likely to go along if only to avoid getting on our bad side. I was confident when I flew down for a meeting but very anxious and nervous. There was always the overhanging thought of opening a nearby new shop to compete, which I never even suggested, but the possibility was obvious. A new store would likely be no more successful but might negatively impact the existing ones. They typically brought up that idea as a response to what we'd do if they didn't sign up. After some further conversation, the franchisee signed up for our new franchise agreement. Within a year, everyone resigned, but we lost some twelve months of growth, which compounds, as I was constantly traveling to complete this change.

As it turned out, we stayed in the supply business and lowered our prices, resulting in most franchises still purchasing a majority of their supplies from us. It was easier for them to make one phone call to our area warehouses and order their needs for one delivery and one bill, and we therefore made a bit more profit in the whole process. In addition, franchisees knew our suggested products were excellent and of the highest quality at very fair prices.

Chicken Delight was a major franchisor whose owner was the first IFA president, a quality businessman, but they took their approximately thousand shops in the other direction. They required all purchasing to be done through them, and after being sold to a large NYSE company, Consolidated Foods, I believe they ended up out of business due to a class action lawsuit, part of which involved the requirement to purchase certain paper and other products.

Mister Donut was built one franchise at a time. We did not allow any multiple-store chains or subfranchises. A sub-franchise would allow the buyer to sell units in the area sub-franchised for a portion of the initial fee and participate in a predetermined percentage of the ongoing royalties (except we did area franchise, as required by Japanese law, for a total one-time fee for Japan and areas of Asia that transferred all Mister Donut rights to them totally). Some twenty-five years ago, we cut the ribbon at the opening of the five-hundredth Mister Donut shop in Japan.

Succeeding in Franchising

Once you cross the line into actually owning a franchise, remember that's not the finish line but the starting line. Now is the time to show what you can really do and perform. Like a racehorse leaving the starting gate, don't go too fast and too hard right from the beginning and run out of energy soon after. Now that you have made a real commitment, understand that it might be a while before you turn a profit. It is crucial to maintain the power of positive thinking when things don't go as planned or unexpectedly go wrong.

Surround yourself with positive people as well and associate with successful businesspeople. Proven leaders in your social network will prove to be extremely valuable to learn from. And read the book *The Power of Positive Thinking* by Reverend Dr. Vincent Peale.

Good, old-fashioned customer service is one of the essential ingredients of franchise success. No matter how much technology makes businesspeople's lives faster and easier, most of all businesses are actually in the people business. Customer service also means hard work—your hard work to improve their experience. Working smarter may be most important. But, in franchising, working harder, working better, and working longer are all requirements to stay ahead and make sure things get done correctly and efficiently.

Franchising is an active team sport. Show and lead by example because if you're not there, one day your company might not be either. Cocktails at 5:00 p.m. are nice, but if you've done nothing or little else, respect is hard to come by. The staff will wake up, and when it really comes time to perform, they won't put out.

And speaking of being in the people business, don't forget your own people. Successful franchises treat their employees as well as they do their customers. Adequate pay, benefits, and training are essential. Hiring the right manager and keeping that person satisfied is one of the main make-or-break ingredients. The franchisee shouldn't be financially superior to his or her supervisors. Mister Donut executives were paid well but, in retrospect, not well enough.

Another not-so-secret secret to success is to study the competition, keeping your eyes open and actually walking through their doors. With apologies to Ralph Waldo Emerson, every franchise is your superior in some way, and you may learn from them. Being aware of your competitors' moves can prevent you from being hurt by their success. Always stay one step ahead and remember that knowledge is power.

All business is about selling, and franchising is no different. Become an expert in sales, whether you're dealing with customers, suppliers, employees, or even your franchisor. Read some of the more popular sales techniques books to learn how to overcome objections and close the deal. All customers at McDonald's are greeted with a happy grin and a cheerful "Welcome to McDonald's" for a reason. This technique is part of what has driven billions of dollars in sales and repeat business.

Don't just leave your accounting to your accountants. Whether you like numbers or not, you must develop an understanding of operating statements of your franchise's results, advising that they should be a quality that accommodates their pay to be higher than those they supervise or sell franchises to.

You will be forced to become a bit of a jack of all trades,

negotiating with a variety of suppliers and managing a diversity of people. To avoid a high employee turnover rate, be courteous and kind to them and pay fairly. Develop a team, and they will build your business.

Case Study: Donut University

One of the best ways to acquire the knowledge to lead a successful franchise is through high-quality training by the franchisor's experts. Mister Donut continuously improved on this concept, opening The Donut University early on to teach its eight-week training program for franchisees. It was a serious education in what was necessary to run a successful franchise. This included long hours covering all aspects of operations, from products and inventory control to baking and management. Significant time was devoted to actual shift taking, featuring on-the-job training in both the back and front of the house, including ordering, bill paying, inventory, and rotating staff training methods and procedures, as well as advertising and marketing.

Donut U offered everything anyone needed to learn to effectively operate, control, teach, market, and otherwise manage a high-volume fast food operation, including donut making. The franchisee was given management control of a real-life operating shop, as staff shared problems they were likely to encounter, including no-show workers, blown fuses, over- or undercooked product, and many other common occurrences.

Also included were research and development labs, consistently trying to improve products, innovate new offerings, and come up with exciting ideas, new items, and even drinks. Muffins were an early addition, as were soups, and we experimented with chocolates, varieties of bakery items, and even hot dogs and a line of sandwiches.

Although we never added chicken to our menu, our product development operations led us to open several fried chicken stores, called The Hatchery, as well as a Mister Donut Jr. shop for secondary (but still active) locations.

In addition to the university, we ran area, regional, and national seminars to showcase our latest ideas, including products, advertising, and marketing. We also presented lectures on the newest operational innovations and brought in suppliers to meet and greet, as well as promote and show what their products could do.

We were too small and too new in the beginning to accomplish executive development. Hiring new and better-quality executives is always a significant difficulty, and long-term loyalty can often get in the way of personnel decisions. Instead, we would create new titles, such as "senior" this or that, which in practice really meant we were replacing the longer-term executive with a newer one. Sometimes we would instead move executives we liked, but still wanted to replace, into a franchise store with a deal they could not refuse.

McDonald's started from scratch, hiring only into the store level. From there, an individual grew to become a store manager before moving into other management areas. Every CEO started as a store manager before rising up through the ranks.

7
Running a Franchise

I have been involved in the franchise world running a wide variety of businesses, from donuts and coffee to high fashion and dental services, and can tell you from experience that they are all basically similar when it comes to franchise execution.

In the end, the franchisee must be involved in every aspect of the day-to-day operation to keep everything running smoothly. Attention to detail is essential, and nothing is too big or too small to be overlooked.

Logical, common-sense efforts that anyone would use to run a successful business apply in the franchise world as well, starting with hard work, setting an example as a leader, knowing your business, being a good delegator and trainer, and following proven company formulas for success. Try to remain positive and constructive as things inevitably go wrong and set an example for your employees to keep the work environment upbeat. Management must lead by example, and your passion and enthusiasm will serve as inspiration for those around you.

Mister Donut franchisees had no need to reinvent their own way of making a cup of coffee. We developed our system through research, training, and trial and error to maximize quality, freshness, and profits. Some franchisees were annoyed at having to toss unused coffee away to maintain only fresh pots or tried to inject less jelly in their filled donuts. However, they bought into an established system, and there were proven reasons to stick to the plan. Cutting corners was the road to disaster, not just for them but everyone.

Following the company's tested directives and proven methods and being a team player was the order of each day. Don't be afraid to talk to the franchisor concerning your needs because they want you to succeed, and nothing is worse for a franchisor than your failure. Maintaining a quality working relationship with the franchisor is essential. Just like any important relationship, this is accomplished through cooperation and communication that hopefully is a two-way street.

All Mister Donut supervisors were assigned to areas containing about twenty stores, which were regularly visited. Sometimes franchisees could consider it interference, but the supervisor's job is to see that quality, cleanliness, and service is maintained. So mind your mentors!

Keep your eyes on the prize, meaning make sure you watch the money, both cash and product. This can be taken literally, watching that employees aren't stealing from you. Delivery quantities should even be monitored. All of your bills should be handled on a regular basis while continually monitoring the cash flow and inventory of the business. To continue to succeed, improvements and repairs should be constant.

Always remember that you are in the customer service business. Especially in this Internet age when everybody is a critic online, and social media sites such as Facebook make commentary by the general public instantaneous to friends and family, the cliché saying that "the customer is always right" couldn't be more important. Satisfied customers tell their friends about your business, and word of mouth is the best (and least expensive) form of advertising. The public is the lifeblood of any business, and reputation counts. Offer customers the opportunity to supply feedback and you may learn some valuable lessons relatively painlessly. Rewarding repeat customers makes them feel special and like they're part of an inside club, and that keeps them coming back and telling their friends. Knowing what your customers want is the only way to keep them satisfied and coming back for more.

Get involved in your community and let people get to know you as a person. You are the iconic face of your business, and people like knowing who is running the show. The manager and owner of any small business should be available to hear compliments as well as complaints. Frequenting your store is the message of satisfied customers who otherwise don't stop by to tell you how much they like you, but those with a gripe often speak out.

Networking inside and outside your location brings in more business and helps introduce and grow a new franchise and sustain a presence. The franchises that last in their communities tend to be the ones that give back, such as Ben Cohen and Jerry Greenfield of Ben and Jerry's Ice Cream. Sponsor youth sports teams, charities, and other things you believe in, if they are within reach of your budget. Don't think of these types of things as unnecessary expenses but proven ways to promote your business at small cost. Making a difference in the surrounding neighborhood fortunately builds customer loyalty.

Case Study: Donuts to High Fashion with Yves Saint Laurent

Selling donuts or high fashion is the same thing when it comes to running a franchise, and that's the basis of the success of the model (and this book). I am living proof.

In 1990, my company became Yves Saint Laurent franchisees of their Rive Gauche line, led by my wife, Barbara. For a decade we were transformed into front-row fashionistas in Paris. My wife had been an aficionado and consumer of the high-fashion world and displayed a keen eye for taste and interest in fashion design. We had no special experience to go into this new retail business. Nothing but casual knowledge of retailing and a buyer's sense and instincts. And that's the point. That's why we put our money on franchising—because we knew we would receive expert guidance. My belief in the franchising system once again proved to be the best way to enter a business without learning everything on our own.

We purchased the exclusive rights to open retail boutiques selling Yves Saint Laurent's Rive Gouche products, arguably the best-known fashions designed at that time in the world, in multiple United States cities. In fact we created famous shops in Boston; Short Hills, New Jersey; and Dallas. We also had the rights to the rest of the country for any region that wasn't open to that date, as well as first refusal rights on existing stores that were resold.

Mr. Yves Saint Laurent designed everything. This made it even easier than donuts from our perspective.

A famous, world-renowned interior designer, selected by YSL but otherwise unavailable to the single boutique owner, designed all their stores. My wife was the buyer for all of our boutiques, receiving advice from the boutique managers she had chosen as well as from YSL. There was always a professional manager Barbara selected for each store to run the day-to-day operations. For example, in Boston she chose as manager the former head of couture of a major upscale department store.

The women who wear Yves Saint Laurent's Rive Gouche are loyal to that design, think they look best in those fashions, and kept coming back each season, serving as repeat customers, just like the donut and coffee patrons at Mister Donut. Obviously, we were dealing with a totally different product line, clientele, and price point, even different types of staffs, but the principles were exactly the same. The outlet sells the cheeseburger, or the muffler, or the evening gown, but business is still business.

Although dealing with flour suppliers and various product representatives of Mister Donut was similar to dealing with the House of Yves Saint Laurent, there was one huge difference that made opening a YSL boutique an enormous risk. There was only one Yves. If he was right in his design judgment, the sales were good, and fortunately he was rarely wrong—that is until sickness, and eventually death, overcame him, and all the franchisees closed up throughout the world. Most franchises lost a significant amount of their investment when they closed.

This represents a very different lesson to learn, but such situations are few and far between, even in fashion. Now other great designers are usually chosen to take over when famous designers die, and perhaps the beat can go on, just as Yves Saint Laurent took over after the death of Christian Dior. That could be happening with YSL today but too many years too late for us.

Inventory and Supplies

One of the significant benefits a franchisor offers is pricing/costs on merchandise and supplies, due to the size and combined volumes multiple units provide.

According to the franchise agreement, specific proprietary (secret) formula items, such as the secret syrup for Coca-Cola, may be required to be purchased directly from the franchisor or as it dictates. Although certain standards must be met on many non-proprietary items, they usually can be purchased from other suppliers as well, as long as the standards are maintained. Some franchisors provide a pre-approved list of suppliers that are acceptable but still warn against substituting other suppliers. Why? Take coffee cups, for example. They can leak, or the lids may not be secure. The logo printed on the outside may not be sharp enough or otherwise perfect, and the cup thickness, per franchisor standards, may not adequately protect from burning the customer. These issues apply across the board to nearly all products.

These requirements used to be among the biggest areas of controversy for franchisees because they sensed they were being taken advantage of by abuses in the pricing of such products. Today, most products are purchased through franchisee cooperatives with franchisor support with no income generated for the franchisor.

You should also arrange regular off-hour deliveries to avoid conflicts with patrons doing business and distracting staff and always leave the best parking spaces for paying customers. Make certain to monitor exactly what is being delivered before you sign off on the items and check that new inventory is stocked appropriately, away from existing, to avoid potential spoilage, among other problems like theft.

You should learn about maintaining inventory during your training, but it is crucial to keep an eye on the store's stockroom. Items not requiring refrigeration are called dry storage, even though they are sometimes not really so dry. Keep such inventory off the ground and away from contamination of anything, including water. Poisonous items and food are obviously a deadly combination; therefore, everything should be well labeled, with date of delivery and expiration clearly notated, and secured with lids. Cleanliness is essential with dry and refrigerated items. Finally, the refrigerator and freezer temperatures need to be monitored and well maintained. All equipment must be regularly inspected and operating properly.

Developing Marketing

One of the glories of being a franchisee is that marketing is usually developed and arranged by the franchisor or a franchisee co-op and perfected through use and trial and error. Use this to your advantage in developing your own specific marketing plan for your individual needs, paying strict attention to the rules and regulations of the system.

The marketing proposition is simple: identify your customers' needs and then figure out how to satisfy them. Marketing includes nearly everything to please the consumer, such as advertising, promotion, publicity, sales, customer service, store design, and signage. A good plan will help direct and coordinate all of your firm's marketing efforts, will identify the potential market, and will present the tactics to attract customers. A marketing plan doesn't need to be a lengthy or expensive proposition but is more about careful thought and research.

Begin by examining your marketplace, including what your competition is doing. Then set realistic goals, budgets, and deadlines for meeting the needs to maximize them. A mission statement helps to focus the strategy, and a clear concept of how results will be measured quantifies the situation.

A good plan begins by describing the business and an analysis of the situation you are in. Define your customers and how to most effectively reach them within your budget.

High-Tech Tips

Modern technology has offered franchisees the ability to keep track of their business even while they are not on location. Most aspects of the business can now be monitored online on laptops, smart phones, and tablets, from streaming video to cash register sales and spreadsheets. Training updates and seminars are even available from the comfort of your own home through video webinars. This ability to be in more than one place at a time has also led to franchisees to better oversee multiple locations simultaneously and franchisors to maintain contact with their locations. Even in mammoth operations, computers have streamlined automatic inventory control and produce ordering.

Common Franchise Pitfalls

No matter how well a franchise system is designed and has worked elsewhere, there is no absolute guarantee of success. Obviously there are even some among both franchisees and franchisors who become rotten apples, and there are those who fail for more valid reasons. Nothing is foolproof.

As emphasized, the most common shortfall for new businesses is not having adequate working capital on hand, particularly in the crucial first year or two of operation. The financial requirements in the Financial Disclosure Document are important to review, but you should always have more cash on hand for unintended unknown problems and emergencies. Problems can occur nationally and internationally, at work and at home simultaneously, requiring an instant infusion of cash or forcing closure. Hope for the best but always be prepared for the worst—and then some.

Competition is fierce and won't disappear. You must stay a step ahead because new innovations will always arise.

Franchisees who don't receive the proper training that they require are more destined to fail than their counterparts. Whatever shortfalls exist must be eliminated. A one- or two-week crash course for a business neophyte will probably not do the job properly.

Don't forget that your family, some of whom may need to participate periodically, must feel satisfied with your new endeavor, too, and support your effort. Bring them into the discussion as early as possible. If your family is miserable with the lifestyle a new business brings with it, the intense negativity will bring you down eventually as well. Just because a business is financially successful does not equal automatic happiness.

Even in the best franchise relationship, as in life in general, conflicts are bound to occur. According to a Griffth University study, 18 percent of franchisees did not feel they received proper information from their franchisors up front, 28 percent did not trust their franchisor, and 36 percent did not think conflict resolution was handled promptly and timely. Legally binding conflict resolution should be part of the original agreement to maximize the impact of this situation.

Although many issues may come down to how well your investigation and due diligence was performed, never assume that you have any rights that are not clearly written out in the documents you sign. Item 11 in the FDD should be read carefully to understand exactly what you would receive from your franchisor.

But with all the good will that exists, misunderstandings are actually normal and will happen. Just don't assume they're intentional. Franchisors, however, don't want disagreement. It hurts them in nearly every way you can imagine, so they'll be as receptive as you to straightening out any problems, if possible.

Just because a franchise system is growing quickly, don't assume that it is actually profitable for each of the franchisees or the franchisor. It shouldn't surprise anyone that franchisors plan to grow rapidly, but franchisees, in general, are far less aggressive. Even successful owners may not, and usually don't desire to, open additional units. They're satisfied with their profits and are not looking for more. In reality, they have different outlooks from franchisors. Quiznos and Krispy Kreme are two popular chains of many that ran into trouble when they began expanding too rapidly. But there are many more franchisors that grew rapidly successfully.

Although new systems offer the opportunity of getting in on the ground floor and buying more cheaply, be careful if you are a beta tester and all of the kinks may have to be worked out at your expense. Since one of the main advantages of buying into a franchise is that it is a tested business model, serving as a guinea pig for a business to work out their details through trial and error (keyword: error) can result in dire consequences. The franchisor must prove through example that it is even possible for a franchise to turn a profit.

It may sound overly negative to begin a new business venture thinking about getting out, but most successful business owners develop an exit strategy early on. You might be extremely satisfied and stay right where you are for many decades until retirement, but one day you will at least likely want to sell the business you have worked so hard to build. Will it be to a family member or an outside individual? What if there are health issues or other reasons to suddenly stop working? These are the types of questions that might need to be asked years in advance to ensure proper planning. Being part of a franchise chain provides assurance that franchisors want your store to continue operating.

Going into any business means accepting the possibility of numerous risks, but by understanding foreseeable risk, it is possible to avoid many common mistakes. That is, in fact, the very basis of successful franchising.

When Partnerships Go Bad

Like a marriage, most business partnerships start off with the best of intentions, but as time goes on sometimes problems arise, and they may sour. There is really no way to protect yourself from the possibility. Think of it like some sort of a marriage pre-nuptial agreement or partnership document. You must hope for the best but prepare for the worst.

The best solution is to avoid potential problems in advance by mapping things out with your partner before the business is even begun. Sit down with a potential partner and write out your mutual expectations of each other. This is kind of an informal, pre-partnership agreement and will also save you considerable time prior to meeting with an attorney.

The most important decision in a partnership is choosing a good partner. Just because someone is a friend or even an experienced expert doesn't make him or her a good partner. Trust your instincts and look for someone with the right professional temperament. It's best to avoid partnering up with people with huge, swollen egos, who think emotionally and have other assorted insecurities. Business is easiest when it is handled calmly, rationally, and thoughtfully and is well planned.

Spell out the details and don't be overanxious about rushing forward to the more glamorous aspects of opening your business. Details of the plan should include partner contributions of money, time, duties, and skills. An established buy-sell agreement in the beginning will avoid a judge determining the value of your share of the company in the end.

Speaking of which, get your lawyer into play early in the game. Bring informal written notes from your expectation discussions along and have the attorney write them up in more official, binding language. The objective, trained, and specialized advice of the professionals you hire early on, such as lawyers, accountants, and managers, will prove invaluable.

Once you hit the brick wall of irreconcilable differences, keep calm and avoid fighting. If things have been properly laid out in advance, a binding mediator can usually iron out most disagreements. The key word here is "compromise," and the only way to achieve that is through calm negotiation. This is far more desirable than the system of last resort: the courts.

Sometimes the problem, like with any marriage, comes down to toxic communication. At that point a professional facilitator could help involved parties to hear each other's grievances and come to a friendly working resolution.

When problems are driving you crazy and you are considering splitting, ask yourself whether the business is successful enough and has enough future growth potential that it's worth saving and working things out, or is it time to walk away? But as Neil Sedaka said in his famous song, we all know that "Breaking Up Is Hard to Do."

If you do split, will you need to solicit outside cash to keep the business running properly? How much? Should you sell out to your partner or buy him/her out? Are you better off walking away entirely, and would it be cheaper to start an entirely new business? Who gets custody of current employees?

This could get messy, so make sure you are certain you can't work through these problems and you are really doing what serves you and your wallet the best. If there is no viable alternative then by all means bring in the mediator, and perhaps it's time to call your attorney to protect yourself and get the best deal possible.

Politics and Franchising: A Lethal Combination

Although politics has no place in franchising, misguided political partisans seem to make headlines regularly by interjecting their viewpoints in between their fried chicken or pizza sales. It's a detrimental combination that will certainly alienate some of their potential customers.

Business is business, so why in a country that's divided between red and blue states would you want to anger about half of your possible customers? Keep your opinions where they belong: in the voting booth! While there's nothing wrong with supporting legislation that may help your business, why get involved in hot-button issues? People are passionate about such topics, and your contradictory views may anger them enough to take their business elsewhere.

Some recent controversy surrounding fast food giants tossing their viewpoints into the ring of public opinion were broadcast endlessly over the cable news networks. Fast food chain Chick-fil-A's chief operating officer, Dan Cathy, created a virtual media firestorm during the 2012 election cycle when he made public statements opposing same-sex marriage. What did this have to do with selling chicken? Obviously nothing at all. While he had the right to state his opinions, that didn't make it right from a public relations or business standpoint.

The company's charitable organizations donated millions of dollars to various similar-leaning political organizations. This led to protests and boycotts for the chain, and certain business partners severed their ties with the company. A counter-protest was also launched with a Chick-fil-A Appreciation Day. Finally, Chick-fil-A was forced to do damage control by releasing a statement in July 2012 that said, "Going forward, our intent is to leave the policy debate over same-sex marriage to the government and political arena." Good advice that would have avoided much controversy if headed off sooner.

Papa John's chief executive, John Schnatter, criticized President Barack Obama's health-care law in a pre-presidential election statement in 2012, stating that he believed it would raise pizza costs by fifteen to twenty cents each. By November, political supporters were organizing a Papa John's Appreciation Day, but who needs this controversy, and what good could it possibly do for selling pizzas?

Other examples include Denny's franchise owner, Jon Metz, announcing a 5-percent "Obamacare surcharge" in November 2012, forcing company CEO John Miller to apologize a few days later. In another example of shortsightedness, Zane Tankel, owner of forty New York Applebee's, told the Fox Business Network that he was hesitant to expand because of the health-care changes during that same time.

I too had my feathers clipped after the assassination of President John F. Kennedy. I had ten-foot posters of the president sent to all stores for display in their front windows in conjunction with a contribution to the Kennedy Library of a day's profits. In hindsight, I should not have been so surprised when some franchisees wouldn't display the pictures or participate in the offering of a day's profits to the library. I hadn't realized then that what I viewed as an act of citizenship would be viewed by some others through a political lens.

Political foot-in-mouth disease seems to have also extended into the 2012 election period. Some franchise leaders could have benefited from keeping their eyes on what was best for their businesses' public relations and sales and less on political messages.

Hiring and Training Staff

Hiring your staff is one of the final steps to getting your new business up and running. The key to good staffing is training, and since they will represent you to the general public, this should not be taken lightly or treated as an afterthought.

They need to be trained not only for their duties but, if they are to meet the public, on how you would like them to act, greet, serve, and all round attend to customers. If you don't, you will need to live with their concepts or imitations of other employees, none of which you may agree with or even like. The better you do this preliminary training, the more likely you will approve of the results. Successful employees are happy employees, resulting in better performance for all.

For the average retail business, there will usually be adequate staff available. Recessions, for example, hit everywhere from time to time but more as macro events than local. Since, in general, the local retail employee is nearer the end of the skill line as compared with the top, there will be a normal supply available. As employees get laid off from higher-level jobs during down times, an even larger supply of workers seeks out whatever job they can get. At such times there will be more part-timers available as they continue to look for the level of job they usually prefer. In good times of low unemployment, there are still staff available who want part time work or second or third jobs and spouses seeking to augment their incomes.

You will find an adequate job market in your location, since by the definition of retail you will be located in a densely populated area, close to public transportation and where people congregate.

Your franchisor and their training manual will help in the initial stages to determine how many people you will need and what positions must be filled. They will also help provide concise job descriptions as you advertise and conduct your search, and the human resources section of their operations manual will offer a great deal of pertinent material. These materials also include interview preparation and profiles of what you should be looking for with each position.

There are many ways to find employees, from a sign on your store to local newspaper advertising, Craigslist, and even word of mouth. Other employees might also refer people they think might be interested. Employment agencies and recruiters could also be useful for some top-level positions, as well as networking with people already in the existing franchise system who might be relocating or otherwise seeking new opportunities.

Like every other aspects of your business, this is another opportunity to sell yourself. Let prospective employees know why they should want to work for you.

It's also important to note that it is your legal responsibility to follow equal opportunity guidelines when hiring employees. Become very familiar with discrimination laws regarding hiring, promotion, and firing, and make sure the language used in advertising for employees conforms to government guidelines. These rules and regulations are strictly enforced by the United States Equal Employment Opportunity Commission (EEOC) and include discrimination due to race, age, disabilities, and gender, as well as enforcement of the Immigration Reform and Control Act.

When conducting interviews, begin by introducing yourself and explaining your business. Keep your questions related to the job and allow potential candidates ample room to explain who they are and why they could be a good potential employee. The only dumb question is the one you didn't ask. These are the people you could be working with for a long time to come and could very seriously affect your success and thus your investment, so select wisely and make sure they are the types of individuals that you want to be associating with on a day-to-day basis. Train them carefully and thoroughly how best to represent you and do their jobs well.

Make sure the potential candidates know exactly what will be expected of them if they are selected and be certain they are an overall good fit. Lay out the complete job description, including their hours, responsibilities, wages and benefits, dress code, and any relevant policies.

Follow up on those that are at the head of the pack by checking their references and running a basic background check. That's become a lot easier with Google and Facebook just a click away, as well as professional background checking websites.

You will also learn as you go by watching the people who prove to do the best at each job. Future hiring should prove easier and more intuitive.

The Captain of the Ship

As the skipper, you must lead your crew through the sometimes-rough waters of your business but with the guiding light of the franchisor serving as your beacon. Once again, the help you receive from the system you bought into should prove invaluable.

You set the tone of your workforce from the top down. The way you dress, act, and carry yourself will be directly reflected by all of your staff. It's not as much what you say as what you do, so be aware that you are always leading by example. Fortunately, by now you've been well trained, so it's time to perform.

You own it, so act the part and set the example for all to follow. Everyone who participates in a great performance is proud to have played his or her role. For your best results, lead the way to this source of pride.

The rules are simple, so follow what's been laid out for you by the corporate big wigs. That's why I've never been thrilled with hiring MBAs to own franchises. They might be well educated business-wise but not better at the small stuff, the day-to-day nitty gritty, and they can be too anxious with their own ideas for important modifications.

Part of being a good manager is being a good jack of all trades. If you are not an expert in whatever needs to be done, you soon will be. But your job, first and foremost, is to manage those around you. It is also important to cross-train many on staff so that they can handle each other's jobs in the event of an emergency, health issues, or the inevitable no-shows. Don't allow anyone in your orchestra to ever miss a beat, never mind fall apart if one or more people suddenly disappear.

Staff training never ceases since employees are usually changing regularly in many franchises. In addition, a good manager must stay on top of new techniques and ideas and continually retrain him- or herself with the main franchise, bringing those techniques back home to pass on to their staff.

Eventually your current employees can begin training the new employees, with you in a supervisory position. Franchisors often have techniques to help train your employees as well through manuals, onsite one on one, or Internet programs. If you are the one expected to do the staff training, the franchisor will usually show you how to do it.

Once you find and train topnotch employees, you'll probably want to hold on to them. Now it's not just a matter of keeping the customer satisfied but the employees as well. With all the time you've already put in to finding the right people, it's important to find ways to show your appreciation and keep them on board. Make sure they understand what's expected of them and offer opportunities for regular feedback. We all need to feel respected and recognized for what we do.

If employees get bored doing their jobs, it will eventually show in their work. To avoid this, a plan of job rotation concerning repetitive mundane tasks can often prove very beneficial when a staff member doesn't make it to work.

Lastly, it is the franchisee's responsibility to keep their employees physically safe in the workplace. Most companies provide guidelines, but you must also review the Department of Labor's Occupational Safety and Health Act. Although most safety items are commonsense procedures, they are also important from a business perspective as well.

Working the System

Being part of a franchise network can be a lot like being part of a big business family. If you learn the rules of the game and play well together, everybody can function to their highest abilities. The opposite is also true: not playing by the rules results in chaos and acrimony. You could also fail in your business and lose your franchise in the process. If you are an extremely creative person and think you can do it better then franchising isn't really for you. You don't buy a Picasso and then change the colors.

You are a cog in a bigger machine in this system, and you must meet the standards supplied by the franchisor. You also have a responsibility to your fellow franchisees to follow the system's plan since your unit also reflects on them. If a customer has a bad experience in your store, he or she may never set foot again into another such place or may even sully the chain's reputation by bad-mouthing the company. In today's Internet world, bad news spreads and, like wildfire, can easily torch the franchise's good name.

Fortunately, mistakes and bad apples are quickly picked from the bunch by a good system with a hardworking field support staff. Working for the franchisor, they deal directly with the franchises on a regular basis. The main goal is to be a sort of "guardian angel" to each franchise, helping out as problems arise and trying to avoid them as they come along the horizon.

Through the field consultants' regular onsite reviews, they can spot what standards are not being properly met. Some franchisors barely check in on their franchisees, however, while others border on micromanagement. Sometimes these could be scheduled visits, but surprise visits at unusual times to find out what's really going on can often reveal quite a bit more. Reviews can also occur without a field visit through statistics and bookkeeping records submitted to the main office electronically.

Franchisors can also be a little secretive, sending clandestine representatives into your place of business to see how things really operate. You can never tell the difference between them and regular civilians when they are in stealth mode, so always treat the customer right.

Your franchisee brethren are also a valuable source of feedback. No unit is an island (to coin a phrase), and whatever problems or questions you might have were most likely already experienced and solved elsewhere in the chain. This is one way in which you can feel like you are part of a veritable team. The system works best if each franchisee serves as part of the team. Many franchises offer advisor councils and associations, where franchisees can gather to exchange ideas and experiences and help each other out in a variety of ways.

In a perfect world, your relationships should be built on mutual respect, with each player doing what he/she does best and learning from others with more knowledge and experience. The franchisor-franchisee relationship is complicated and, like any relationship, metamorphosizes over time. The needs of a new unit are quite different from a seasoned multi-unit group. Neither side can rest too long on its laurels and must continually move forward to keep the other satisfied. It's starting to sound a lot like a marriage again, isn't it?

Franchisors do everything they can to gain and keep the cooperation of the franchisee. They will plead and jawbone, but, in the end, if a franchise is hurting the chain and the public by a consistent lack of cleanliness and quality, they can be put in a spot to take legal action. Fortunately, to protect the public, courts are sensitive. It is a last resort, but the hammer exists and has been brought down with success most of the time.

To stay ahead of the competition, franchises must continually invest in research and development. Times and tastes change, seemingly more rapidly all the time. Individual stores may be used to test new products, and the franchisee's detailed and honest appraisal report is crucial to moving a product line forward. Hopefully, the bosses have done thorough research and testing before any new item is released, reducing the risk level overall, but ultimately it is a trial-and-error business. By having the resources of a large chain behind you, the marketing attempts are not resting only on your shoulders, but the burden is spread throughout.

On the other hand, some franchisees contribute creative ideas that expand the system as a whole. One example that resulted from franchisee experimentation is serving breakfast at a hamburger restaurant that otherwise didn't open until just before noon, considerably increasing revenues and profits for everyone. Some businesses even grew into twenty-four-hour operations and stayed open on holidays and weekends, when they were formerly closed.

Managing Conflicts

Once again good communication is the key to a healthy franchisee-franchisor relationship. From time to time things may occur that you may think are negative toward you or your business or where you disagree with the franchisor's opinion or criticism. Calm discussion and compromise are usually the best approach. Litigation should almost always be the means of last resort for resolving conflicts.

The Customer Is Always Right

Dealing with the general public means keeping a smile on your face through the good, the bad, and the ugly. Always remember that customer feedback is now instantaneous online, and those who have not enjoyed the experience of your franchise can spread the word quickly through social media networks like Facebook and Yelp.

There are many times you will also be dealing with negative, nasty customers. In these scenarios, being right isn't necessarily the end game; keeping the customer satisfied should be. Sometimes this will just prove impossible no matter how hard you try and how many hoops you offer to jump through, but where possible it makes much more sense and is ultimately more rewarding.

This is one of the reasons being a hands-on franchisee pays off. By literally keeping your eyes open, you can spot problems as they happen, maybe even nip them in the bud, and deal with unsatisfied customers on the spot. Listen to their complaints completely and avoid unnecessary interruptions since most rational people calm down once they feel they have been heard. Be polite as they speak, even if they occasionally resort to harsh tones and words, and always keep a smile on your face while maintaining eye contact. Empathy goes a long way, so try to put yourself in the position of the customer.

Once the problem is properly diagnosed, offer to remedy the situation on the spot if possible and include some sort of perk. This can include a discount coupon or something free to make the consumer feel special and bring him/her back again.

Feedback is an essential means of quality control, so make customer comment cards readily available and take the time to read them. If the complaint makes sense then you should respond quickly. Your franchisor has probably heard similar complaints, so feel free to contact them to see how such things were handled before, if applicable.

Marketing Basics

By jumping onboard a proven system, you have the distinct advantage of inheriting an already established marketing plan. One of the primary functions of this style of business is the existing brand recognition. But it doesn't stop there, so don't sit back and let the big boys handle it all. This is your business we're talking about. These proven networks also often offer recommendations of what you can do on your turf to better establish yourself.

In general, franchisees don't usually want to get involved in marketing. Some systems require that advertising programs all initiate at the top. That makes sense since they control and protect the brand name. In these cases there's not much to do as an individual, and since you are paying for the overall advertising budget, simply observe the experienced masters at work.

If you can advertise your individual location then the franchisor probably already has proven ad ideas available for you to use, as your budget sees fit. There are countless local media outlets of all types available to place your message with, from old-school newspaper, radio, and television to state-of-the-art websites and social marketing tools like Facebook and Groupon.

Advertising techniques are evolving in today's multiplatform world and are beyond the scope of this book, but some basics might help you better spend your budget. Repetition is better than just a big splash. If all you can afford is one full-page advertisement in a newspaper, consider four quarter pages in four consecutive issues instead. People need to see the name of the business over and over, hopefully eventually compelling them to come in and sample your product.

Media buying is in distress in recent years, so always haggle over the rate. The rate card offered to you is usually just a starting point, and discounts are available for everything from paying in cash in advance to multiple insertions. Most media outlets have a lot of space or airtime for sale and usually have limited markets to fill them.

It's also important to manage your expectations and not to expect immediate results. In the same way that your corporate bosses branded their products over the years, you must brand your location. Sometimes advertising is just for name recognition and establishing yourself, without any direct sales correlation.

However, don't just throw advertising money against the wall without monitoring its actual effectiveness. Coupon discounts are a great way of doing this. If there is an influx of coupons from certain advertising sources, those are the best destinations for future dollars. Many local advertising sources are ethically challenged when it comes to reporting their real circulations, claiming wild numbers for newspapers thrown on top of cigarette machines in diners, etc. A coupon in their paper will quickly quantify the effectiveness of advertising with them. Always ask to see verification of their circulation, viewers, or listeners.

Sometimes there is a local-national hybrid model, where franchises in a specific area can pool their resources for a bigger-discounted advertising buy. Keeping a focused message in front of such a local audience is mutually beneficial.

Other promotional opportunities include sponsoring a little league team with your name emblazoned on uniforms for all to see. Follow up with press releases to local media outlets about your team and make sure to include quality photos. Local charities often need assistance with promotions, which can also put you in a good light within the community. Cross promotions with other local business are also an idea that can prove to be mutually beneficial.

Telemarketing, newsletters, direct mail, blogs online, and videos on YouTube are all forms of promotion that are relatively inexpensive yet keep your name in front of your potential audience.

Always consult with your franchisor before undertaking any promotion or advertising venture. Not only will you usually need their prior approval, but they can also provide quality materials for your use, including pre-made ad campaigns, logos, photos, and text.

8

Growing as a Franchisee

Now that your franchise is a proven, thriving success, it's time to look toward the future and consider opportunities for expansion. The ringing cash register has proven you can do it, so now is the time to strike while the iron is hot and discuss with the franchisor the possibility of your opening more locations. Before you make the jump, understand that there are risks involved with spreading yourself too thin. The hands-on approach that made your initial venture so successful could actually be the downfall of your next.

The upside is that owning more units can mean making substantially more money. The downside is that it is also an opportunity to fail and lose your shirt. You might be successful enough that the franchisor approaches you about opening more franchises, but you must research your opportunities as thoroughly as you did the first time around.

For a franchise veteran, certain opportunities for financing and increased purchasing power may now exist that weren't available before. You might even be offered real estate locations without even having to go out looking because of your proven track record. Finding employees is probably easier, and if you need to swap them out between locations for any reason there is more opportunity as well. Your best employees can also help run the new enterprise and train the new arrivals, taking some of the burden off of you.

Another option is partnering up with a new franchisee, where you bring your expertise to the table while your partner can be more hands-on. This way you are also taking less of a financial risk yourself.

Before you move forward with any form of expansion, make sure it is practical for you in terms of time and money and is not just your ego talking. Being a mogul is fine but not if it breaks your piggy bank or destroys your existing business.

The first step to growing bigger, however, is to make sure it's even allowed under your current franchising agreement. There are franchises that will only allow a person to own one unit. Also crunch the numbers with your accountant to make sure you can even afford what you are possibly getting yourself into. Don't drain your current business dry just to launch another.

New skills will also be required to pursue multiple units. Since you can't possibly be in two places at one time, you must learn to delegate authority. Managing one store is more of a hands-on operation, while multiple units require a complete support network.

Many of the issues of a startup can be avoided by purchasing an existing franchise from someone seeking to move on. Make certain you understand the reasons they are looking to bail out of their operation before you jump in since it could be the result of unforeseen problems. There are also some times when company-owned locations are available for sale.

Acquiring a competitor's location and turning it into your brand is yet another possibility. When Mister Donut was acquired by Allied Domecq, which then also owned Dunkin' Donuts, Allied quickly merged the two chains, changing the Mister Donut signage and coloring to Dunkin's motif, adding valuable market share of some 50 percent while simultaneously both illuminating essentially an entire management organization and removing their major competitor.

Some franchisors also offer the opportunity of master franchising, or the right to develop an entire area where you control a certain number of units within a specific geographic region. Often this comes with the right to sell franchises to others within that area, effectively making you a subfranchisor. Now you're really entering mogul territory and should receive a percentage of the sales for these new units but usually for a heavy down payment.

Once you've caught the franchising bug, opportunities also exist to bring other brands on board. Once again you might be restricted in which other businesses you can participate in under your franchising agreement. Beware, though; starting from scratch with a new brand will take even more time from your original franchise than adding multiple units in the first place. Now you have to negotiate and learn an entirely new system.

Your franchisor will probably be asking how you intend to manage both simultaneously, if you're even allowed to proceed in the first place, and you better have some good answers. If your experience and skill set will somehow make multiple franchises thrive in a stronger way, perhaps bringing business in from a companion business next door, then explore further.

Many franchisors are consolidating and buying different brands or starting new concepts to complement their existing business. Dunkin' Brands now operates Dunkin' Donuts, Baskin-Robbins, and Togo's, often under one franchise roof. Mrs. Fields Famous Brands includes Mrs. Fields Cookies, TCBY, Pretzel Time, Great American Cookies, and Pretzel Maker. As you can see, there are many opportunities to expand under the same parent company.

You may decide to go with a new franchise if there is no

room to grow with your current enterprise for a variety of reasons. You also may wish to diversify or see upcoming problems with your exiting business.

When more than one brand operates under the same roof, it is called co-branding. This is growing more popular and makes for greater shopper convenience. This can mean all operations are owned by one franchisee, or maybe a large retail space is shared by multiple franchisees.

Co-branding can also be accomplished by taking in a partner of a complementary brand, either as strong as your current franchise or even stronger. Don't get dragged down by an inferior product riding your established coattails. Your current site might be reconfigured, if space and franchise agreement allows, or perhaps a new location must be built from scratch. Certain expenses and staff might be shared to reduce the overall costs of running the operation.

Your Exit Strategy

Before you even begin operating your franchise, you should already be considering your exit strategy. This might not occur until you are ready to retire but could come much earlier for a variety of financial, family, business, and health reasons, including simple burnout.

Since a franchise agreement is limited in time, at some point it will be time to say good-bye. The things that will make a store more successful are great quality, cleanliness, and service, and there is no other or better exit strategy than selling a successful business.

Depending on your original agreement, you will likely have different options at the end of your lease. One is to sign on for an additional period to continue operating your business, or it can possibly be sold. Often the terms of such renewals are specified in the original contract, so be certain to review carefully, even though they might not kick in for decades. Fees are often less for renewals because everything is not starting from the ground up, and you are now a proven commodity. The new agreement you will be offered will likely look quite different from the previous one you signed since the company will have evolved in many ways as the years passed and the chain grew. Fees may change, territories may expand or contract, and you may be required to remodel, retrain, or add new equipment and signs.

Although you can't always time your exit, it will likely pay to get out while the getting is good. A good economy will bring more buyers to your door, as will lower interest rates and more-available financing. This includes the local economy, right down to the very block you are on, all the way up to the national and perhaps global economic scene. The industry you are in might have its own ups and down that need to be taken into consideration when timing a sale.

The success of the franchisor itself can also be a significant bargaining chip. When a certain franchise is red hot, much like a good stock, it is a good time to cash in your chips. Bad press, poor reputation, or sinking stock prices may hit you in the pocketbook as well when you are looking to sell. Networking with other franchisees can be a good way to discover the current value of your unit, and they may actually be interested in purchasing what you are selling.

The best way to make a smooth transition out of your business, a strong coda to your franchise symphony, is to begin the process early. A rushed job usually brings negative consequences with it.

If you are seeking to sell a business, be certain the books are in order and hopefully show a nice profit. Although you need to always keep good financial records, all of the details must be properly recorded when a potential buyer is going over them with a fine-tooth comb.

Just like when you sell a home, you must present your business in the best light possible. That can include simple things like a fresh coat of paint or perhaps some upgraded equipment. That first impression can be crucial. Rest assured that you have already taken care of one of the most difficult and important aspects of a sale: the location of the property. This one is locked in stone and may have an overriding effect on the eventual sale price. Hopefully, you have chosen your spot wisely and values in the area have gone in your favor. Your value will be higher the more time you have remaining on your agreement.

After all the blood, sweat, and tears you've put into building your business, you certainly value it highly. But keep personal prejudices aside and try to objectively and accurately determine the value for a sale. Ultimately it is only worth what someone is willing to pay. Pushing the sale price too high will force it to just sit on the open market, while you will feel like a sucker if you sell too low.

There are franchise brokers out there who will devise a mathematical formula for you based on profit and sales, but valuations should also be based on growth potential and the condition of the industry and economy. A proper independent appraisal of your business is usually worth the expense. For a company worth under $2 million, the valuation appraisal cost is approximately $2,500 and takes about a month.

The franchisor could be a great help in determining your sale price as well. They would know how much similar units in comparable areas have been selling for and may even have possibly interested clients already lined up. They usually will not set an exact price, however, due to potential legal liabilities over potential conflicts of interest.

Transferring franchise ownership will also probably require the new franchisee to sign an agreement with the parent company, so life is a little more complicated than selling your own business.

Finally, your franchisor usually has final approval over whom you sell to; after all, it's their reputation and future at stake. Don't assume that just because your son wants to take over the business it can just happen. Training and experience would be an important prerequisite for such scenarios.

The franchisor usually has the right of first refusal with any sale, so they may instead choose to buy it from you themselves, based on the same terms as the prospective buyer. Check the terms of your agreement to see how long a franchisor can take to use this clause. This also may affect the sale, since aware buyers know that the option may exist.

The franchisor likely will also receive a small transfer fee to cover its expenses when the sale is made to an outsider. This is why it pays to stay in the loop with your franchisor through the course of your agreement to learn how they tend to handle such sales so there are fewer surprises when the time comes for your own exit.

In *The Godfather Part III*, Michael Carleone says, "Just when I thought I was out…they pull me back in." The franchise business may prove the same once you sell out. Unless they have truly entered retirement, many franchisees get that itch to jump back in the game soon after they sell, joining a new franchise network or opening a new franchise of the same system in a different area. This is a good opportunity to relocate your life while taking your expertise with you. Franchisors will value your knowhow when you seek to open a new branch.

Becoming a Franchisor

First and foremost, your business must already be a rousing and sustained success, highly profitable with reasonable return on investment and easily replicated. Is the market already saturated with similar enterprises? Are you bringing something fresh and new to the table? All of the things we looked for when studying purchasing someone else's franchise apply to building your own empire.

Most of the kinks have to be worked out of your prototype before you even consider offering it to others. Others will not want to serve as your beta testers with their hard-earned money. Your brand must be recognizable and have established consumer demand and profit.

Becoming an expert at your own business does not necessarily mean you are ready to become a franchisor. You need to develop a different outlook and skill set first. All of the things franchisors offer need to be developed by you or, more likely, by an experienced management team hired by you. This team will help you develop a quality Franchise Disclosure Document that will hopefully impress potential franchisees.

All of these things take money, and, like with starting any new business, significant working capital will be required to get this off the ground. How much will it cost to properly develop a sellable system? If becoming a franchisor will take you away from your existing business, you may be effectively killing the goose that laid the golden egg. In addition to the launch, you must be able to finance continual training programs as well as research and development.

If all of the basics we've been discussing on these pages so far are in place, becoming a franchisor should be relatively easy. In fact, it's a lot simpler to operate and to keep things running smoothly and profitably than it is to develop and execute a franchise system. Once you've got the operations down pat, most of the staff is interchangeable, except in a restaurant (the chef, baker, or similar expert). Otherwise, whether in the back or front of the house, staff members are fairly interchangeable if need be, and their skills, for the most part, are available at a cost that is on the modest side. Of course there are exceptions, but this is generally the norm.

On the other hand, the unique positions needed within a franchising operation that require a good amount of expertise are considerably more expensive and harder to find. For example, financial and accounting are wholly different for a franchisor. The accounting systems are not basic bookkeeping positions, as they are for franchisees. Rather, they require considerable broader financial expertise. It's one thing to be a bookkeeper in a factory, for example, doing the same posting or bill paying day in and day out, but another to be the controller or financial vice president responsible for all accounting and all bookkeepers and clericals. The chief financial officer is responsible for nearly everything: buying, research and development, and negotiating business arrangements and contracts.

With a franchisor, the directors of franchise sales, marketing, advertising, legal, engineering, real estate, construction, research, training, and more are usually not interchangeable, except to a small degree in the franchise sales and marketing areas, and require significant knowledge and experience. Therefore, it is often advisable to bring in an independent expert to evaluate your dreams and walk you through the process of becoming a franchise mogul. Consultants can be found at the IFA's supplier forum.

If you are determined to go it alone, you are likely in for an uphill battle. Although some of the legal documents may be boilerplate-like, they are best handled by experts to avoid future problems. If you can't afford to hire the proper professionals at this stage, this might be a warning sign that you're not properly capitalized to be a franchisor yet.

There are many so-called experts out there pretending to be franchise packagers, only looking to take advantage of dreamers at this vulnerable point in their careers. Beware of such sharks swimming in these dangerous waters. Research their client list and check referrals and make sure the people you are dealing with are certified professionals, lawyers, accountants, etc. with documented proof of their experience in the franchising world. They might sell the illusion of making it easy to become a franchisor but beware—you don't want to face problems with regulators down the road.

These advisors and consultants are very much worth their expense. They've been there and done that. They are like coaches on a sports team, having gone through the positions and played the game, with good luck and bad breaks. They make a great deal of difference, at comparatively little cost, because the money they'll keep you from losing is likely to be considerably greater than whatever they are paid.

The best way to find the finest experts is through the recommendation of established franchisors and franchisees and the IFA's supplier forum. Review those recommendations in detail, online and with the American Bar Association Franchising Forum. Follow up by meeting a select list in person and find out what they will actually do for you.

Once your team members are in place, they can help you map out a (hopefully) winning strategy for success. Attorneys will have detailed checklists they have developed dealing with similar scenarios over the years and can guide you each step of the way. A detailed, structured business plan can then be properly prepared and implemented, including writing up all of the necessary legal and promotional documents.

Above all, don't be in a mad rush to expand your business. Take your time and do it right so it can grow properly and safely into the future, and money doesn't go pouring down the drain before you can keep up with the knowledge and plans you are accumulating.

Winning Ideas

The most important thing is coming up with the Big Idea. Most of the best are obvious…once you've seen them become successful. You can wait for lighting to strike, or you can try to conjure one up yourself. Places to seek inspiration include solving an existing problem, also described as "necessity is the mother of invention."

Don't let the high-tech success of recent college dropouts make you give up if you haven't earned your first million dollars before you can even legally drink. Most successful entrepreneurs are, in fact, actually middle-aged people who have learned through the school of hard knocks and invest their own hard-earned money to start up their dream business.

There are almost an infinite variety of good business ideas out there, but the ones that succeed have one thing in common: management perseverance. Many companies fail because entrepreneurs give up before they have a chance to succeed, so don't be afraid of failure. You will never succeed if you don't fail on the road to get there. The evolution of a failing company can sometimes lead to an amazing success. Your customers will tell you what works, if you listen. Pivot quickly and morph your company into something better.

Don't listen to the negativity around you. Everyone from family and friends to so-called industry experts will offer their advice as to why your business will fail. You cannot succeed if you take no for an answer. First, you must believe in yourself and your idea.

Finding Franchisees

Just because a person might be ready to plop down a franchise fee does not necessarily make someone a good choice to be a franchisee. They must be prepared to competently meet all of the criteria we have previously discussed. This is someone who will be representing your business, so choose wisely. There are also a limited number of franchisees for each market, and overselling devalues the other units.

Understand your potential markets thoroughly. Does your product play equally in urban and suburban areas? Will it sell in the Midwest and/or on the coasts? Investigate ways to market to your most desirable potential clients.

For example, the farther west one goes in our country, customers order a cup of coffee darker. In Boston, a regular coffee is light and has cream and sugar, while in California a regular coffee is black, no cream or sugar. In between, the regular goes from light to darker to black.

Determine which qualities your potential franchisees should have and then actively market to them. A screening process early on can prevent time-wasters who aren't serious with their inquiries or are completely unqualified or even just thinking of stealing your idea. The Internet is a great place for leads, with the highest-percentage lead-generation of any marketing device, but since it is such a Wild West mentality in the cyber world, there will be a high percentage of fishing expeditions without any real fish. *The Wall Street Journal* used to be the best, and is still very good, for franchise leads.

Franchise sales brokers and trade shows will bring in a much higher percentage of qualified candidates, as will franchise directories and publications. Referrals from trusted sources generate the most reliable leads and the highest percentage of returns.

Your sales tools should be ready for marketing your franchise opportunity, from websites to printed brochures and press kits. Operations manuals, various forms, support networks, fee structure, legal issues, and training programs need to be ready to go. Without the total package, with the complete documents ready to go, the pace will be slow and the results uneven.

At Mister Donut, not only did we have a 100-percent complete package, we literally wouldn't change a word in our franchise contract. The franchise prospect and the lawyer would be told this in advance. This is truly a take-it-or-leave-it sale. How would you like it if you, as a franchise prospect, were aware that everyone else had different deals, and yours was, or might be, the worst? Don't sign it. No changes. Now, that doesn't apply to a new change or changes everyone from a given date forward receives. That change is universal and appropriate and represents growth and better knowledge.

Successful franchisors build up a department specializing in franchise recruitment and sales. That's all they think about, twenty-four hours a day. The best person to lead such an organization would be someone with a great deal of past experience growing a similar unit. They already understand the system, inside and out, and can convey the subtle nuances to perspective clients with expert authority and confidence. This person can take a client by the hand and walk them through the entire process, creating a trusted comfort zone.

Someone from your growing legal or accounting department

should serve as compliance officer to sign off on the deals developed by the salesperson. Their expertise should already have been established through the course of building the operation.

Begin the process with a lower member of your staff pre-screening an applicant, moving quickly when interest is shown. They should follow up with printed material and links to appropriate web pages and then follow up with an appointment to speak in person at a "discovery day" meeting at your main office. This is where you open your virtual kimono to reveal your Franchise Disclosure Document details, if you haven't already done that at the first meeting.

Soon after meeting day, follow up with viable candidates by checking their backgrounds, résumés, and finances. Inform candidates whether they passed the test and will be welcomed into your business family. After the appropriate waiting period, it's time to try to ink the deal.

Breaking the International Market

Expanding across the globe offers another set of special needs. Are you ready to be an international business mogul? First determine whether your product or service will get lost in translation, remaining unknown or unappreciated in outside areas with different languages, rules, and customs. If you thought this game was complicated up until now…just wait. There's a litany of rules and regulations, as well as complicated international laws, differing for each country.

Make sure your system is an American success before you even attempt to try it elsewhere. The first thing to ascertain is if your system is even translatable to other cultures. Sometimes things will work with modifications. McDonald's had great difficulty when entering France, developing more easily in other

European countries. Remember Vincent Vega's classic line of dialogue in *Pulp Fiction*? "A Big Mac's a Big Mac, but they call it '*le Big Mac*.'"

Costs will be different from market to market and region to region, such as supplies and labor and rent and construction costs. Demographic research will help determine if there even is a market for your product or service in each country, but you will really only learn this fact from actual operations. And such a transition will cost considerable money to pull off, from lawyers, accountants, and other experts to various administrative assistants.

In Canada, we were told we had to have tea and serve it in a pot and that Canadians weren't coffee drinkers. The facts were that we sold little tea and eventually eliminated it, and coffee sales were larger per Canadian store than stores in the United States. At that time, coffee in Canada was a poor product. Mister Donut coffee, promoted as "The World's Best Coffee," was, in fact, special. Canadians loved the product, and we expanded very rapidly in Canada.

In our expansion to Japan, we found rents so much higher that we had to take less than usual space. That meant a change in the size and availability of equipment, which would impact sales and baking hours and quantities per batch. Fortunately, volume was so great that none of that mattered, including less sweetness for the taste of the Japanese.

It may seem glamorous to become an international jet-setter. But can your business model accommodate another layer of expenses? Consider partnering up with native experts to make your job easier. Or perhaps arrange an area franchise allowing subfranchising with a major company. And, remember, you'll be involved in a foreign currency where exchange rates fluctuate constantly.

International franchising could easily take up another

book; this mention is like a dip of your toe into foreign waters. The IFA also offers international trade missions, and the annual International Franchise Exposition brings in many potential foreign franchisees. Local chambers of commerce and embassies can also be of help in foreign countries for networking and information.

Another opportunity is becoming a franchisee in the United States of a foreign franchise. There are many new difficulties to face when considering this alternative that are similar to what was discussed in bringing an American franchise to foreign soil. The initial dilemma is: will it work on foreign soil? Like Mister Donut in Japan, it may work even better.

Conclusion

"Your time is limited, so don't waste it living someone else's life. Don't be trapped by dogma—which is living with the results of other people's thinking. Don't let the noise of others' opinions drown out your own inner voice. Most important, have the courage to follow your heart and intuition. They somehow already know what you truly want to become. Everything else is secondary."
—Steve Jobs

"Twenty years from now you will be more disappointed by the things you didn't do than by the ones you did do. So throw off the bowlines. Sail away from the safe harbor. Catch the trade winds in your sails. Explore. Dream. Discover."
—Mark Twain

Now that you have officially become an honorary franchise expert by reading this book, it's time to make your entrepreneurial dreams come true and go for it. Create your own future and live the dream. The number-one cause of not fulfilling your potential is fear of failure. But for some of those who can get over that fear, success awaits.

Don't be discouraged by the naysayers surrounding you or the doom and gloom of the financial press. Franchising isn't for everybody, but if you believe in your heart that you should own your own business, now is as good a time as any to start.

Do a thorough self-examination to determine if you've got what it takes in terms of drive and initiative and what I've always emphasized the most: stick-to-itiveness. It helps too if you have the financial means to pull it off. If you and your family agree then it's time to leave your safety zone and dive into the deep waters of a new and exciting life. It certainly won't be easy but can be rewarding for many, as it has always been.

Are you ready to be your own boss? Then begin by reaching out to franchisors that intrigue you and, when and if you find a "turn on," take the plunge. Do your due diligence until the right one rings a bell. Don't expect overnight success and your trials and tribulations—and hard work—will likely be rewarded. The timing couldn't be better, with our economy needing good jobs, money and financing plentiful, and government resources available.

Welcome to a new life, and good luck as your own boss: a business owner in the franchise world.

www.ingramcontent.com/pod-product-compliance
Lightning Source LLC
Chambersburg PA
CBHW061652040426
42446CB00010B/1710